Richard Green Moulton

Bible Stories

(Old Testament)

Richard Green Moulton

Bible Stories
(Old Testament)

ISBN/EAN: 9783337100346

Printed in Europe, USA, Canada, Australia, Japan

Cover: Foto ©Lupo / pixelio.de

More available books at **www.hansebooks.com**

The Modern Reader's Bible

Children's Series

Old Testament Stories
New Testament Stories

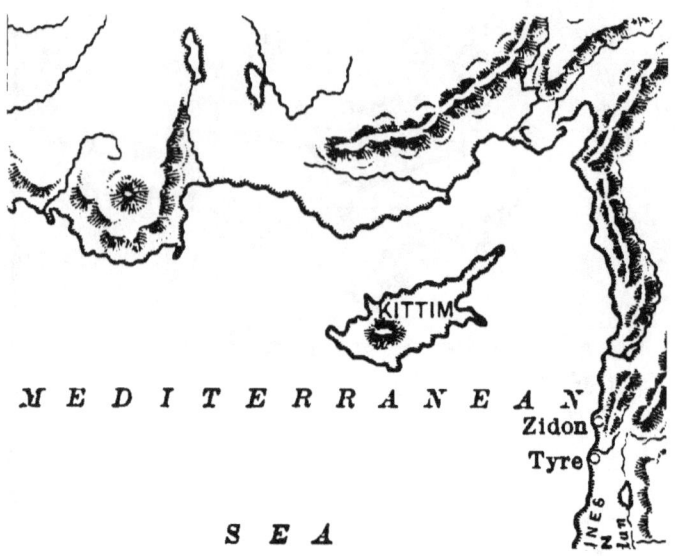

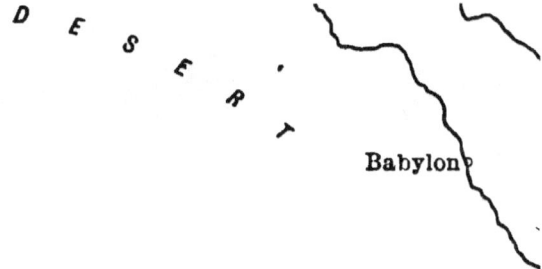

Map of the
OLD TESTAMENT WORLD

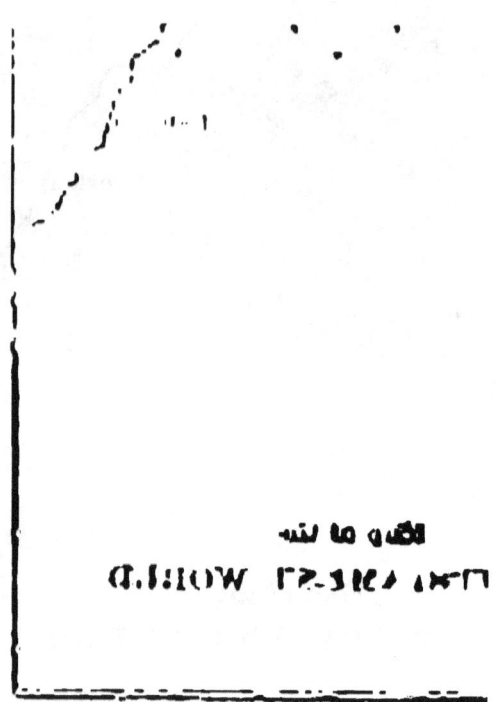

العالم ما بنى
CLAIM WORLD

THE MODERN READER'S BIBLE

A SERIES OF WORKS FROM THE SACRED SCRIPTURES PRESENTED IN MODERN LITERARY FORM

BIBLE STORIES

(OLD TESTAMENT)

EDITED, WITH AN INTRODUCTION AND NOTES

BY

RICHARD G. MOULTON, M.A. (CAMB.), PH.D. (PENN.)

PROFESSOR OF LITERATURE IN ENGLISH IN THE
UNIVERSITY OF CHICAGO

New York
THE MACMILLAN COMPANY
LONDON: MACMILLAN & CO., LTD.
1899

All rights reserved

COPYRIGHT, 1899,
BY THE MACMILLAN COMPANY.

Set up and electrotyped January, 1899. Reprinted June, 1899.

Norwood Press
J. S. Cushing & Co. — Berwick & Smith
Norwood Mass. U.S.A.

PREFACE

THIS is announced as a Children's Number of the Modern Reader's Bible. The term 'Children' covers a wide variety of capacity, from an intelligence greater than that of many adults to a child mind that needs to be addressed in a language of its own. The text of this volume is suitable for all; the introductions and notes are intended for older children, or for others only by transmission through the minds of parents and teachers.

The stories which make the text are in the language of Scripture, altered only by omissions. The Bible has this amongst other marks of a classic: that its language has the power of attracting young minds, even where (in the opinion of their seniors) the subject matter ought to be beyond them. As in the other volumes of the Modern Reader's Bible, I follow the Revised Version, with frequent substitutions of margin for text: for the use of this I express my obligation to the University Presses of Oxford and Cambridge.

The volume is arranged according to the natural divisions of Bible history: Genesis, The Exodus, The Judges, The

Preface

Kings and Prophets, The Exile and Return.* Each period is represented by its most important stories; the purpose of the introduction and notes to each section is to weave all together by indicating briefly the bearing of each story on the general history. Thus it is hoped that the whole volume may leave on a young mind an impression of Old Testament history, in outline complete (however scanty), but with outline supplemented by the most vivid picturing of important points. With the selection of stories no one will be satisfied, least of all the editor. But those who may be inclined to be censorious on this subject should try the experiment of making a selection themselves, and they will see how an editor has to sacrifice his own favourites to stern limitations of space and suitability.

There can surely be no question that these classic stories of Biblical literature should have a place in all education, whether of the home, the Sunday School, or the instruction that calls itself secular. The inquiry is sometimes made, how such literature should be used in practical teaching. I would say that our first duty to a story is to love it: nothing in the way of discussion is legitimate that interferes with the prerogative of the young mind to absorb story and to reproduce it in its own way. With the observance of this limitation I would suggest that the next use of such stories as these is to light up portions of ancient

* Each of these five parts (Introduction, Text, and Notes) can be obtained separately, in paper covers, price 15 cents each.

Preface

history; I have endeavoured to give help in this way by the introductions and notes. Again, the literary charm of Scripture narrative is so great that these stories will serve where nothing more is desired than a reading book. More than this, it is the function of story to bring up persons and incidents with the vividness of present reality: they lend themselves to moral and religious comment, which thus becomes a comment on life itself. In the present case, such commenting must be left to parent or teacher: the notes of this series go no further than assisting towards the appreciation of each incident as a piece of literature.

I may be permitted a word on the relation of this to other volumes of the Modern Reader's Bible. The present, and its companion volume of New Testament Stories, are intended as ground plan of Bible history: the separate sections correspond to the separate volumes of the History Series in the larger work. When, in the story form, the ground has been covered as a whole, then some particular section may be chosen for study in the full form of history, story, documents, which make up Bible history as it stands. Similarly, the volume entitled *Select Masterpieces of Biblical Literature* is intended to introduce to all varieties of literary form represented in Scripture, and its sections correspond to the various series — History, Wisdom, Prophecy, etc. — into which the Modern Reader's Bible is divided: after all forms have become familiar in type, some one series can be selected for continuous study, the volumes

Preface

of the series being arranged in the proper order, while the introductions to each volume bring out the unity of the series as a whole. Thus to cover a general field by vivid selections, and then pursue a restricted part of it with fulness of detail, is the sound order of study.

R. G. MOULTON.

CONTENTS

GENESIS

	PAGE
Introduction	3
i. The Creation of the World	7
ii. The Temptation in the Garden of Eden . . .	10
iii. Cain and Abel	12
iv. The Flood	13
v. The Call of Abraham	18
vi. The Birth and Offering of Isaac	19
vii. The Wooing of Rebekah	23
viii. How Jacob stole the Blessing from his Brother .	29
ix. The Story of Joseph and his Brethren . . .	35
Joseph and his Brethren in Canaan . .	35
Joseph as a Slave in Egypt	38
How in one day Joseph passed from a Slave to a Prime Minister	42
Joseph and his Brethren in Egypt . . .	46
The Journey of the Children of Israel from Canaan to Egypt	58
Notes to Genesis	61

Contents

THE EXODUS

		PAGE
Introduction		69
i.	Moses and the Plagues of Egypt	73
	The *Wonderful Preservation of Moses as a Babe*	73
	The Ten Plagues of Egypt	74
	The Overthrow of the Egyptians at the Red Sea	88
ii.	Law of the Ten Commandments from Sinai . .	95
iii.	The Witness of Balaam to Israel	98
Notes to the Exodus		107

THE JUDGES

Introduction		113
i.	The Passage of the Jordan and Siege of Jericho	119
ii.	How the wily Gibeonites deceived Joshua .	122
iii.	War of Deborah and Barak against Sisera .	125
iv.	Feats of Gideon in the Midianite War . .	133
v.	The Story of Jephthah's Vow . . .	139
vi.	Stories of Samson	142
	Samson's Wedding Feast	142
	The Jawbone of an Ass	144
	Samson and Delilah	146
	Death of Samson	148
vii.	The Old Man Eli and the Child Samuel . .	149
	Birth of Samuel	149
	The Child Samuel called to be Prophet . .	151

Contents

		PAGE
	Loss of the Ark and Death of Eli	153
	The Return of the Ark	155
viii.	The Anointing of Saul	159
ix.	The Rejection of Saul and Anointing of David	167
x.	The Feud of Saul and David and the Friendship of David and Jonathan	172
	David and Goliath	172
	How the Feud and the Friendship began	177
	The Escape by Night	179
	The Secret Meeting of David and Jonathan	181
	The Adventure of the Spear and Water-cruse	185
	The Battle of Gilboa	189
Notes to the Judges		193

THE KINGS AND PROPHETS

Introduction		201
i.	David and the Prophet Nathan	207
ii.	The Revolt of Absalom	209
iii.	The Wisdom of Solomon	215
iv.	Story of the Divided Kingdom	219
v.	Stories of the Prophet Elijah	221
	Elijah and the Prophets of Baal	221
	Elijah in the Desert	227
	The Story of Naboth's Vineyard	229
	Ascent of Elijah to Heaven	232
vi.	Stories of the Prophet Elisha	234
	The Shunammite's Son	234
	Naaman and Gehazi	237

Contents

		PAGE
vii.	The Assyrian Army and the Prophet Isaiah	241
viii.	King Josiah and the Finding of the Law	247
Notes to The Kings and Prophets		250

THE EXILE AND RETURN

Introduction		255
i. Stories of the Captives in Babylon		259
The Burning Fiery Furnace		259
The Dream of the Tree that was cut down		263
Belshazzar's Feast		268
Daniel in the Den of Lions		272
ii. The Story of Esther		275
How a Jewish Maiden became a Queen		275
Haman's Wicked Plot and how it was overthrown		278
Mordecai Prime Minister of the Empire		286
iii. Stories of the Return		290
How Nehemiah rebuilt the Walls of Jerusalem		290
The Renewal of the Covenant under Ezra		299
Notes to The Exile and Return		307

Rough Map of the Old Testament World

BIBLE STORIES

GENESIS

INTRODUCTION TO GENESIS

The stories which make up this volume are a part of the History of the People of Israel, as given by themselves in the books of the Bible. This people of Israel (also called Hebrews or Jews) is one of the greatest races of the world in regard to its history and literature; moreover, it is through this people that we who live today have received our holy religion.

Bible history is unlike other history. It is not a mere narrative of events: everything is put forward with one purpose. This purpose is to proclaim how Israel is a Chosen Nation, having a mission to represent God to the other nations of the earth. Thus, while their God is the God of the whole earth, yet Israel is a 'Covenant People.' This means that there is a covenant between God and the Chosen Nation, by which He is in a very special sense their God, and they have a special obligation to bear witness for Him to the rest of mankind. An old English word for 'covenant' is 'testament': hence the 'Old Testament' is the Covenant of God with his ancient people Israel. Whether we are reading the full history of the Bible or these stories selected from it, we should always bear in mind this main thought of God's Chosen People and their mission.

Introduction   ⇥ Bible Stories

The first part of the history is called 'Genesis'; that is, 'Origin.' It describes the formation of the Chosen Nation. They had not yet become a nation, but were in what is called the 'patriarchal stage': that is, they had no national government, but, like the different branches of a family, looked to the authority of the fathers (or 'patriarchs') for their rule. We should have expected such a history to begin with the earliest of these 'patriarchs'—Abraham. As a fact, however, Genesis goes further back in time, in order to bring forward two earlier examples of covenants between God and men. After relating the Creation of the World, the history tells of a covenant made by God with Adam and Eve. The story of the Temptation in the Garden of Eden shows how this covenant was broken, and man was driven out of Eden. The sin thus commenced grew worse, as we see by the story of Cain and Abel. Then we are told of the Flood, and the destruction of a world grown wholly sinful; after this God made another covenant with Noah and his descendants. These two covenants were made with Adam and Noah as ancestors of all mankind: the next story tells of the Call of Abraham to separate himself from the rest of men, with the promise that he should be the father of God's special people.

It must have seemed at the time as if this promised nation would never come into existence, for Abraham and his wife Sarah grew into years without any children. Hence the prominence of the story which relates the Birth

Genesis   Introduction

of Isaac in Abraham's old age. Again, while Isaac was still a youth, his life, on which so much depended, was all but brought to an end, not through disease or accident, but by a voluntary offering up of Isaac in sacrifice at the command of God. At the last moment he was saved from death: and this whole incident brings out how Abraham's descendants were a people consecrated to a sacred purpose.

The story of the Wooing of Rebekah shows the care taken in the selection of a wife for Isaac, worthy to be the mother of the great people to come. To Isaac and Rebekah were born two sons, Esau and Jacob: the strange story of the Stolen Blessing shows how the younger supplanted the elder as ancestor of the coming nation.

This Jacob, afterward named 'Israel,' had twelve sons, ancestors of the twelve tribes in the future nation. Most of these children of Israel led an obscure shepherd life. But one of them, Joseph, appears to have been a man of strong character and great powers. After a life of strange adventures, Joseph at last became ruler of Egypt under its king Pharaoh. The famous story of Joseph and his Brethren is the natural close of Genesis, for it brings the Children of Israel into Egypt—then one of the world's greatest empires—and in this Egypt the next stage of their existence was to be passed.

Stories from Genesis

   i. The Creation of the World
  ii. The Temptation in the Garden of Eden
 iii. Cain and Abel
 iv. The Flood
  v. The Call of Abraham
 vi. The Birth and Offering of Isaac
vii. The Wooing of Rebekah
viii. How Jacob stole the Blessing from his Brother
 ix. The Story of Joseph and his Brethren
      Joseph and his Brethren in Canaan
      Joseph as a Slave in Egypt
      How in one day Joseph passed from a Slave to a Prime Minister
      Joseph and his Brethren in Egypt
      Journey of the Children of Israel into Egypt

i

The Creation of the World

IN the beginning God created the heaven and the earth. And the earth was waste and void; and darkness was upon the face of the deep: and the spirit of God moved upon the face of the waters.

And God said, Let there be light: and there was light. And God saw the light, that it was good: and God divided the light from the darkness. And God called the light Day, and the darkness he called Night. And there was evening and there was morning, one day.

And God said, Let there be a firmament in the midst of the waters, and let it divide the waters from the waters. And God made the firmament, and divided the waters which were under the firmament from the waters which were above the firmament: and it was so. And God called the firmament Heaven. And there was evening and there was morning, a second day.

And God said, Let the waters under the heaven be gathered together unto one place, and let the dry land appear: and it was so. And God called the dry land Earth; and the gathering together of the waters called he

The Creation ᛞ **Bible Stories**

Seas: and God saw that it was good. And God said, Let the earth put forth grass, herb yielding seed, and fruit tree bearing fruit after its kind, wherein is the seed thereof, upon the earth: and it was so. And the earth brought forth grass, herb yielding seed after its kind, and tree bearing fruit, wherein is the seed thereof, after its kind: and God saw that it was good. And there was evening and there was morning, a third day.

And God said, Let there be lights in the firmament of the heaven to divide the day from the night; and let them be for signs, and for seasons and for days and years: and let them be for lights in the firmament of the heaven to give light upon the earth: and it was so. And God made the two great lights; the greater light to rule the day, and the lesser light to rule the night: he made the stars also. And God set them in the firmament of the heaven to give light upon the earth and to rule over the day and over the night, and to divide the light from the darkness: and God saw that it was good. And there was evening and there was morning, a fourth day.

And God said, Let the waters bring forth abundantly the moving creature that hath life, and let fowl fly above the earth in the open firmament of heaven. And God created the great sea-monsters, and every living creature that moveth, which the waters brought forth abundantly, after their kinds, and every winged fowl after its kind: and God saw that it was good. And God blessed them, saying,

Genesis   The Creation

Be fruitful, and multiply, and fill the waters in the seas, and let fowl multiply in the earth. And there was evening and there was morning, a fifth day.

And God said, Let the earth bring forth the living creature after its kind, cattle, and creeping thing, and beast of the earth after its kind: and it was so. And God made the beast of the earth after its kind, and the cattle after their kind, and every thing that creepeth upon the ground after its kind: and God saw that it was good. And God said, Let us make man in our image, after our likeness: and let them have dominion over the fish of the sea, and over the fowl of the air, and over the cattle, and over all the earth, and over every creeping thing that creepeth upon the earth. And God created man in his own image, in the image of God created he him; male and female created he them. And God blessed them: and God said unto them, Be fruitful, and multiply, and replenish the earth, and subdue it; and have dominion over the fish of the sea, and over the fowl of the air, and over every living thing that moveth upon the earth. And God said, Behold, I have given you every herb yielding seed, which is upon the face of all the earth, and every tree, in the which is the fruit of a tree yielding seed; to you it shall be for meat: and to every beast of the earth, and to every fowl of the air, and to every thing that creepeth upon the earth, wherein there is life, I have given every green herb for meat: and it was so. And God saw every thing that he had made, and, behold, it was very good. And there was evening and there was morning, the sixth day.

And the heaven and the earth were finished, and all the host of them. And on the seventh day God finished his work which he had made; and he rested on the seventh day from all his work which he had made. And God blessed the seventh day, and hallowed it: because that in it he rested from all his work which God had created and made.

ii

The Temptation in the Garden of Eden

And the LORD God planted a garden, in Eden. And the LORD God commanded the man, saying, Of every tree of the garden thou mayest freely eat: but of the tree of the knowledge of good and evil, thou shalt not eat of it: for in the day that thou eatest thereof thou shalt surely die.

Now the serpent was more subtil than any beast of the field which the LORD God had made. And he said unto the woman, Yea, hath God said, Ye shall not eat of any tree of the garden? And the woman said unto the serpent, Of the fruit of the trees of the garden we may eat: but of the fruit of the tree which is in the midst of the garden, God hath said, Ye shall not eat of it, neither shall ye touch it, lest ye die. And the serpent said unto the woman, Ye shall not surely die: for God doth know that in the day ye eat thereof, then your eyes shall be opened, and ye shall be as God, knowing good and evil. And when the woman saw that the tree was good for food, and that it was a delight to the eyes, and that the tree was to be desired to make one wise, she took of the fruit thereof, and did eat; and she gave also unto her husband with her, and he did eat.

And they heard the voice of the LORD God walking in the garden in the cool of the day: and the man and his wife hid themselves from the presence of the LORD God amongst the trees of the garden. And the LORD God called unto the man, and said unto him, Where art thou? And he said, I heard thy voice in the garden, and I was afraid; and I hid myself. And he said, Hast thou eaten of the tree, whereof I commanded thee that thou shouldest not eat? And the man said, The woman whom thou gavest to be with me, she gave me of the tree, and I did eat. And the LORD God said unto the woman, What is this thou hast done? And the woman said, The serpent beguiled me, and I did eat. And the LORD God said unto the serpent, Because thou hast done this, cursed art thou above all cattle, and above every beast of the field; upon thy belly shalt thou go, and dust shalt thou eat all the days of thy life: and I will put enmity between thee and the woman, and between thy seed and her seed: it shall bruise thy head, and thou shalt bruise his heel. Unto the woman he said, I will greatly multiply thy sorrow; in sorrow thou shalt bring forth children; and thy desire shall be to thy husband, and he shall rule over thee. And unto Adam he said, Because thou hast hearkened unto the voice of thy wife, and hast eaten of the tree, of which I commanded thee, saying, Thou shalt not eat of it: cursed is the ground for thy sake; in toil shalt thou eat of it all the days of thy life; thorns also and thistles shall it bring forth to thee; and thou shalt eat the herb of the field; in the sweat of thy face shalt thou eat bread, till thou return unto the ground; for out of it wast thou taken: for dust thou art, and unto dust shalt thou return.

So he drove out the man; and he placed at the east of the garden of Eden the Cherubim, and the flame of a sword which turned every way, to keep the way of the tree of life.

iii

Cain and Abel

Abel was a keeper of sheep, but Cain was a tiller of the ground. And in process of time it came to pass, that Cain brought of the fruit of the ground an offering unto the Lord. And Abel, he also brought of the firstlings of his flock and of the fat thereof. And the Lord had respect unto Abel and to his offering: but unto Cain and to his offering he had not respect. And Cain was very wroth, and his countenance fell. And the LORD said unto Cain, Why art thou wroth? and why is thy countenance fallen? If thou doest well, shalt thou not be accepted? and if thou doest not well, sin coucheth at the door: and unto thee is its desire, but thou shouldest rule over it. And Cain told Abel his brother. And it came to pass, when they were in the field, that Cain rose up against Abel his brother, and slew him. And the LORD said unto Cain, Where is Abel thy brother? And he said, I know not: am I my brother's keeper? And he said, What hast thou done? the voice of thy brother's blood crieth unto me from the ground. And now cursed art thou from the ground, which hath opened her mouth to receive thy brother's blood from thy hand; when thou tillest the ground, it shall not henceforth yield unto thee her strength; a fugitive and a wanderer shalt thou be in the earth.

iv

The Flood

Noah was a righteous man: Noah walked with God. And Noah begat three sons, Shem, Ham, and Japheth.

And God saw the earth, and, behold, it was corrupt;

for all flesh had corrupted his way upon the earth. And God said unto Noah, The end of all flesh is come before me; for the earth is filled with violence through them; and, behold, I will destroy them with the earth. Make thee an ark of gopher wood; rooms shalt thou make in the ark, and shalt pitch it within and without with pitch. And this is how thou shalt make it: the length of the ark three hundred cubits, the breadth of it fifty cubits, and the height of it thirty cubits. A light shalt thou make to the ark, and to a cubit shalt thou finish it upward; and the door of the ark shalt thou set in the side thereof; with lower, second, and third stories shalt thou make it. And I, behold, I do bring the flood of waters upon the earth, to destroy all flesh, wherein is the breath of life, from under heaven; every thing that is in the earth shall die. But I will establish my covenant with thee; and thou shalt come into the ark, thou, and thy sons, and thy wife, and thy sons' wives with thee. And of every living thing of all flesh, two of every sort shalt thou bring into the ark, to keep them alive with thee; they shall be male and female. Of the fowl after their kind, and of the cattle after their kind, of every creeping thing of the ground after its kind, two of every sort shall come unto thee, to keep them alive. And take thou unto thee of all food that is eaten, and gather it to thee; and it shall be for food for thee, and for them. Thus did Noah; according to all that God commanded him, so did he.

Genesis   The Flood

In the six hundredth year of Noah's life, in the second month, on the seventeenth day of the month, on the same day were all the fountains of the great deep broken up, and the windows of heaven were opened. And the rain was upon the earth forty days and forty nights. In the selfsame day entered Noah, and Shem, and Ham, and Japheth, the sons of Noah, and Noah's wife, and the three wives of his sons with them, into the ark; they, and every beast after its kind, and all the cattle after their kind, and every creeping thing that creepeth upon the earth after its kind, and every fowl after its kind, every bird of every sort. And they went in unto Noah into the ark, two and two of all flesh wherein is the breath of life. And they that went in, went in male and female of all flesh, as God commanded him: and the LORD shut him in. And the flood was forty days upon the earth; and the waters increased, and bare up the ark, and it was lift up above the earth. And the waters prevailed, and increased greatly upon the earth; and the ark went upon the face of the waters. And the waters prevailed exceedingly upon the earth; and all the high mountains that were under the whole heaven were covered. Fifteen cubits upward did the waters prevail; and the mountains were covered. And every living thing was destroyed which was upon the face of the ground, both man, and cattle, and creeping thing, and fowl of the heaven; and they were destroyed from the earth: and Noah only was left, and they that were with him in the ark. And the waters prevailed upon the earth an hundred and fifty days.

And God remembered Noah, and every living thing, and all the cattle that were with him in the ark: and God made a wind to pass over the earth, and the waters assuaged; the fountains also of the deep and the windows of heaven were stopped, and the rain from heaven was restrained; and the waters returned from off the earth continually: and after the end of an hundred and fifty days the waters decreased. And the ark rested in the seventh month, on the seventeenth day of the month, upon the mountains of Ararat. And the waters decreased continually until the tenth month: in the tenth month, on the first day of the month, were the tops of the mountains seen. And it came to pass at the end of forty days, that Noah opened the window of the ark which he had made: and he sent forth a raven, and it went forth to and fro, until the waters were dried up from off the earth. And he sent forth a dove from him, to see if the waters were abated from off the face of the ground; but the dove found no rest for the sole of her foot, and she returned unto him to the ark, for the waters were on the face of the whole earth: and he put forth his hand, and took her, and brought her in unto him into the ark. And he stayed yet other seven days; and again he sent forth the dove out of the ark; and the dove came in to him at eventide; and, lo, in her mouth an olive leaf pluckt off: so Noah

Genesis &   The Flood

knew that the waters were abated from off the earth. And he stayed yet other seven days; and sent forth the dove; and she returned not again unto him any more. And it came to pass in the six hundred and first year, in the first month, the first day of the month, the waters were dried up from off the earth: and Noah removed the covering of the ark, and looked, and, behold, the face of the ground was dried. And in the second month, on the seven and twentieth day of the month, was the earth dry.

And God spake unto Noah, saying, Go forth of the ark, thou, and thy wife, and thy sons, and thy sons' wives with thee. Bring forth with thee every living thing that is with thee of all flesh, both fowl, and cattle, and every creeping thing that creepeth upon the earth; that they may breed abundantly in the earth, and be fruitful, and multiply upon the earth. And Noah went forth, and his sons, and his wife, and his sons' wives with him: every beast, every creeping thing, and every fowl, whatsoever moveth upon the earth, after their families, went forth out of the ark.

And God spake unto Noah, and to his sons with him, saying, And I, behold, I establish my covenant with you, and with your seed after you; and with every living creature that is with you, the fowl, the cattle, and every beast of the earth with you; of all that go out of the ark, even every beast of the earth. This is the token of the covenant which I make between me and you and every living creature that is with you, for perpetual generations: I do set my bow in the cloud, and it shall be for a token of a covenant between me and the earth. And it shall come to pass, when I bring a cloud over the earth, that the bow shall be seen in the cloud, and I will remember my covenant, which is between me and you and every living creature of all flesh; and the waters shall no more become a flood to destroy all flesh.

V

The Call of Abraham

Now the LORD said unto Abram, Get thee out of thy country, and from thy kindred, and from thy father's house, unto the land that I will shew thee: and I will make of thee a great nation, and I will bless thee, and make thy name great; and be thou a blessing: and I will bless them that bless thee, and him that curseth thee will I curse: and in thee shall all the families of the earth be blessed. So Abram went, as the LORD had spoken unto him; and Abram was seventy and five years old when he departed out of Haran. And Abram took Sarai his wife, and they went forth to go into the land of Canaan; and into the land of Canaan they came.

And when Abram was ninety years old and nine, the LORD appeared to Abram, and said unto him, I am God

Almighty; walk before me, and be thou perfect. And I will make my covenant between me and thee, and will multiply thee exceedingly. And Abram fell on his face: and God talked with him, saying, As for me, behold, my covenant is with thee, and thou shalt be the father of a multitude of nations. Neither shall thy name any more be called Abram, but thy name shall be 'Abraham'; for the 'father of a multitude of nations' have I made thee. And I will make thee exceeding fruitful, and I will make nations of thee, and kings shall come out of thee. And I will establish my covenant between me and thee and thy seed after thee throughout their generations for an everlasting covenant, to be a God unto thee and to thy seed after thee. And I will give unto thee, and to thy seed after thee, the land of thy sojournings, all the land of Canaan, for an everlasting possession; and I will be their God.

vi

The Birth and Offering of Isaac

And the LORD appeared unto Abraham by the oaks of Mamre, as he sat in the tent door in the heat of the day; and he lift up his eyes and looked, and, lo, three men stood over against him: and when he saw them, he ran to meet them from the tent door, and bowed himself to the earth, and said, My lord, if now I have found favour in thy sight, pass not away, I pray thee, from thy servant: let now a little water be fetched, and wash your feet, and rest yourselves under the tree: and I will fetch a morsel of bread, and comfort ye your heart; after that ye shall pass on: forasmuch as ye are come to your servant. And they said, So do, as thou hast said. And Abraham hastened into the tent unto Sarah, and said, Make ready quickly three measures of fine meal, knead it, and make cakes. And Abraham ran unto the herd, and fetched a calf tender and good, and gave it unto the servant; and he hasted to dress it. And he took butter, and milk, and the calf which he had dressed, and set it before them; and he stood by them under the tree, and they did eat. And they said unto him, Where is Sarah thy wife? And he said, Behold, in the tent. And he said, I will certainly return unto thee when the season cometh round; and, lo, Sarah thy wife shall have a son. And Sarah heard in the tent door, which was behind him. Now Abraham and Sarah were old, and well stricken in age. And Sarah laughed within herself. And the LORD said unto Abraham, Wherefore did Sarah laugh, saying, Shall I of a surety bear a child, which am old? Is any thing too hard for the LORD? At the set time I will return unto thee, when the season cometh round, and Sarah shall have a son. Then Sarah denied, saying, I laughed not; for she was afraid. And he said, Nay; but thou didst laugh.

Genesis — Isaac

And the LORD visited Sarah as he had said, and the LORD did unto Sarah as he had spoken. And Sarah bare Abraham a son in his old age, at the set time of which God had spoken to him. And Abraham called the name of his son that was born unto him, whom Sarah bare to him, Isaac. And Abraham was an hundred years old, when his son 'Isaac' was born unto him. And Sarah said, God hath made me to 'laugh': every one that heareth will 'laugh' with me; for I have borne Abraham a son in his old age.

And it came to pass that God did prove Abraham, and said unto him, Abraham; and he said, Here am I. And he said, Take now thy son, thine only son, whom thou lovest, even Isaac, and get thee into the land of Moriah; and offer him there for a burnt offering upon one of the mountains which I will tell thee of. And Abraham rose early in the morning, and saddled his ass, and took two of his young men with him, and Isaac his son; and he clave the wood for the burnt offering, and rose up, and went unto the place of which God had told him. On the third day Abraham lifted up his eyes, and saw the place afar off. And Abraham said unto his young men, Abide ye here with the ass, and I and the lad will go yonder; and we will worship, and come again to you. And Abraham took the wood of the burnt offering, and laid it upon Isaac his son; and he took in his hand the fire and the knife; and they went both of them together. And Isaac spake unto Abraham his father, and said, My father: and he said, Here am I, my son. And he said, Behold, the fire and the wood: but where is the lamb for a burnt offering? And Abraham said, God will provide himself the lamb for a burnt offering, my son: so they went both of them together. And they came to the place which God had told him of; and Abraham built the altar there, and laid the wood in order, and bound Isaac his son, and laid him on the altar, upon the wood. And Abraham stretched forth his hand, and took the knife to slay his son. And the angel of the LORD called unto him out of heaven, and said, Abraham, Abraham: and he said, Here am I. And he said, Lay not thine hand upon the lad, neither do thou any thing unto him: for now I know that thou fearest God, seeing thou hast not withheld thy son, thine only son, from me. And Abraham lifted up his eyes, and looked, and behold, behind him a ram caught in the thicket by his horns: and Abraham went and took the ram, and offered him up for a burnt offering in the stead of his son. And the angel of the LORD called unto Abraham a second time out of heaven, and said, By myself have I sworn, saith the LORD, because thou hast done this thing, and hast not withheld thy son, thine only son: that in blessing I will bless thee, and in multiplying I will multiply thy seed as the stars of the heaven, and as the sand which is upon the sea shore; and thy seed shall possess the gate of his enemies; and in thy seed shall all the nations of the earth be blessed; because thou hast obeyed my voice. So Abraham returned unto his young men, and they rose up and went together to Beer-sheba; and Abraham dwelt at Beer-sheba.

vii

The Wooing of Rebekah

And Abraham was old, and well stricken in age: and the LORD had blessed Abraham in all things. And Abraham said unto his servant, the elder of his house, that ruled over all that he had: I will make thee swear by the LORD, the God of heaven and the God of the earth, that thou shalt not take a wife for my son of the daughters of the Canaanites, among whom I dwell: but thou shalt go unto my country, and to my kindred, and take a wife for my son Isaac. And the servant said unto him, Peradventure the woman will not be willing to follow me unto this land: must I needs bring thy son again unto the land from whence thou camest? And Abraham said unto him, Beware thou that thou bring not my son thither again. The LORD, the God of heaven, that took me from my father's house, and from the land of my nativity, and that spake unto me, and that sware unto me, saying, Unto thy seed will I give this land; he shall send his angel before thee, and thou shalt take a wife for my son from thence. And if the woman be not willing to follow thee, then thou shalt be clear from this my oath; only thou shalt not bring my son thither again. And the servant sware to Abraham concerning this matter.

And the servant took ten camels, of the camels of his master, and departed; having all goodly things of his master's in his hand: and he arose, and went to Mesopotamia, unto the city of Nahor. And he made the camels to kneel down without the city by the well of water at the time of evening, the time that women go out to draw water. And he said, O Lord, the God of my master Abraham, send me, I pray thee, good speed this day, and shew kindness unto my master Abraham. Behold, I stand by the fountain of water; and the daughters of the men of the city come out to draw water: and let it come to pass, that the damsel to whom I shall say, Let down thy pitcher, I pray thee, that I may drink; and she shall say, Drink, and I will give thy camels drink also: let the same be she that thou hast appointed for thy servant Isaac; and thereby shall I know that thou hast shewed kindness unto my master. And it came to pass, before he had done speaking, that, behold, Rebekah came out, who was born to Bethuel the son of Milcah, the wife of Nahor, Abraham's brother, with her pitcher upon her shoulder: and the damsel was very fair to look upon. And she went down to the fountain, and filled her pitcher,

Genesis — Rebekah

and came up. And the servant ran to meet her, and said, Give me to drink, I pray thee, a little water of thy pitcher. And she said, Drink, my lord: and she hasted, and let down her pitcher upon her hand, and gave him drink. And when she had done giving him drink, she said, I will draw for thy camels also, until they have done drinking. And she hasted, and emptied her pitcher into the trough, and ran again unto the well to draw, and drew for all his camels. And the man looked stedfastly on her; holding his peace, to know whether the LORD had made his journey prosperous or not. And it came to pass, as the camels had done drinking, that the man took a golden ring of half a shekel weight, and two bracelets for her hands of ten shekels weight of gold; and said, Whose daughter art thou? tell me, I pray thee. Is there room in thy father's house for us to lodge in? And she said unto him, I am the daughter of Bethuel the son of Milcah, which she bare unto Nahor. She said moreover unto him, We have both straw and provender enough, and room to lodge in. And the man bowed his head, and worshipped the LORD. And he said, Blessed be the LORD, the God of my master Abraham, who hath not forsaken his mercy and his truth toward my master: as for me, the LORD hath led me in the way to the house of my master's brethren.

And the damsel ran, and told her mother's house according to these words. And Rebekah had a brother, and his name was Laban: and Laban ran out unto the man, unto

Rebekah →8 Bible Stories

the fountain. ∫ And it came to pass, when he saw the ring, and the bracelets upon his sister's hands, and when he heard the words of Rebekah his sister, saying, Thus spake the man unto me; that he came unto the man; and, behold, he stood by the camels at the fountain. And he said, Come in, thou blessed of the LORD; wherefore standest thou without? for I have prepared the house, and room for the camels. And the man came into the house, and he ungirded the camels; and he gave straw and provender for the camels, and water to wash his feet and the men's feet that were with him. And there was set meat before him to eat: but he said, I will not eat, until I have told mine errand. And he said, Speak on. And he said, I am Abraham's servant. And the LORD hath blessed my master greatly; and he is become great: and he hath given him flocks and herds, and silver and gold, and menservants and maidservants, and camels and asses. And Sarah my master's wife bare a son to my master when she was old: and unto him hath he given all that he hath. And my master made me swear, saying, Thou shalt not take a wife for my son of the daughters of the Canaanites, in whose land I dwell: but thou shalt go unto my father's house, and to my kindred, and take a wife for my son. And I said unto my master, Peradventure the woman will not follow me. And he said unto me, The LORD, before whom I walk, will send his angel with thee, and prosper thy way; and thou shalt take a wife for my son of my

Genesis — Rebekah

kindred, and of my father's house: then shalt thou be clear from my oath, when thou comest to my kindred; and if they give her not to thee, thou shalt be clear from my oath. And I came this day unto the fountain, and said, O LORD, the God of my master Abraham, if now thou do prosper my way which I go: behold, I stand by the fountain of water; and let it come to pass, that the maiden which cometh forth to draw, to whom I shall say, Give me, I pray thee, a little water of thy pitcher to drink; and she shall say to me, Both drink thou, and I will also draw for thy camels: let the same be the woman whom the LORD hath appointed for my master's son. And before I had done speaking in mine heart, behold, Rebekah came forth with her pitcher on her shoulder; and she went down unto the fountain, and drew: and I said unto her, Let me drink, I pray thee. And she made haste, and let down her pitcher from her shoulder, and said, Drink, and I will give thy camels drink also: so I drank, and she made the camels drink also. And I asked her, and said, Whose daughter art thou? And she said, The daughter of Bethuel, Nahor's son, whom Milcah bare unto him: and I put the ring upon her nose, and the bracelets upon her hands. And I bowed my head, and worshipped the LORD, and blessed the LORD, the God of my master Abraham, which had led me in the right way to take my master's brother's daughter for his son. And now if ye will deal kindly and truly with my master, tell me: and if not, tell me; that I may turn to the right hand, or to the left. Then Laban and Bethuel answered and said, The thing proceedeth from the LORD: we cannot speak unto thee bad or good. Behold, Rebekah is before thee, take her, and go, and let her be thy master's son's wife, as the LORD hath spoken. And it came to pass, that, when Abraham's servant heard their words, he bowed himself down to the earth unto the LORD. And the servant brought forth jewels of silver, and jewels of gold, and raiment, and gave them to Rebekah: he gave also to her brother and to her mother precious things.

And they did eat and drink, he and the men that were with him, and tarried all night; and they rose up in the morning, and he said, Send me away unto my master. And her brother and her mother said, Let the damsel abide with us a few days, at the least ten; after that she shall go. And he said unto them, Hinder me not, seeing the LORD hath prospered my way; send me away that I may go to my master. And they said, We will call the damsel, and inquire at her mouth. And they called Rebekah, and said unto her, Wilt thou go with this man? And she said, I will go. And they sent away Rebekah their sister, and her nurse, and Abraham's servant, and his men. And they blessed Rebekah, and said unto her, Our sister, be thou the mother of thousands of ten thousands, and let thy seed possess the gates of those which hate them. And Rebekah arose, and her damsels, and they rode upon the camels, and followed the man: and the servant took Rebekah, and went his way. And Isaac went out to meditate in the field at the eventide: and he lifted up his eyes, and saw, and, behold, there were camels coming. And Rebekah lifted up her eyes, and when she saw Isaac, she lighted off the camel. And she said unto the servant, What man is this that walketh in the field to meet us? And the servant said, It is my master: and she took her veil, and covered herself. And the servant told Isaac all the things that he had done. And Isaac brought her into his mother Sarah's tent, and took Rebekah, and she became his wife; and he loved her: and Isaac was comforted after his mother's death.

viii

How Jacob stole the Blessing from his Brother

And it came to pass, that when Isaac was old, and his eyes were dim, so that he could not see, he called Esau his elder son, and said unto him, My son: and he said unto him, Here am I. And he said, Behold now, I am old, I know not the day of my death. Now therefore take, I pray thee, thy weapons, thy quiver and thy bow, and go out to the field, and take me venison; and make me savoury meat, such as I love, and bring it to me, that I may eat; that my soul may bless thee before I die.

And Rebekah heard when Isaac spake to Esau his son.

And Esau went to the field to hunt for venison, and to bring it. And Rebekah spake unto Jacob her son, saying, Behold, I heard thy father speak unto Esau thy brother, saying, Bring me venison, and make me savoury meat, that I may eat, and bless thee before the LORD before my death. Now therefore, my son, obey my voice according to that which I command thee. Go now to the flock, and fetch me from thence two good kids of the goats; and I will make them savoury meat for thy father, such as he loveth: and thou shalt bring it to thy father, that he may eat, so that he may bless thee before his death. And Jacob said to Rebekah his mother, Behold, Esau my brother is a hairy man, and I am a smooth man. My father peradventure will feel me, and I shall seem to him as a deceiver; and I shall bring a curse upon me, and not a blessing. And his mother said unto him, Upon me be thy curse, my son: only obey my voice, and go fetch me them. And he went, and fetched, and brought them to his mother: and his mother made savoury meat, such as his father loved. And Rebekah took the goodly raiment of Esau her elder son, which were with her in the house, and put them upon Jacob her younger son: and she put the skins of the kids of the goats upon his hands, and upon the smooth of his neck: and she gave the savoury meat and the bread, which she had prepared, into the hand of her son Jacob.

And he came unto his father, and said, My father: and he said, Here am I; who art thou, my son? And Jacob said unto his father, I am Esau thy firstborn; I have done according as thou badest me: arise, I pray thee, sit and eat of my venison, that thy soul may bless me. And Isaac said unto his son, How is it that thou hast found it so quickly, my son? And he said, Because the LORD thy God sent me good speed. And Isaac said unto Jacob, Come near, I pray thee, that I may feel thee, my son, whether thou be my very son Esau or not. And Jacob went near unto Isaac his father; and he felt him, and said, The voice is Jacob's voice, but the hands are the hands of Esau. And he discerned him not, because his hands were hairy, as his brother Esau's hands: so he blessed him. And he said, Art thou my very son Esau? And he said, I am. And he said, Bring it near to me, and I will eat of my son's venison, that my soul may bless thee. And he brought it near to him, and he did eat: and he brought him wine, and he drank.

And his father Isaac said unto him, Come near now, and kiss me, my son. And he came near, and kissed him: and he smelled the smell of his raiment, and blessed him, and said:

> See, the smell of my son
> > Is as the smell of a field which the LORD hath blessed:
> And God give thee of the dew of heaven,
> And of the fatness of the earth,
> > And plenty of corn and wine:

> Let peoples serve thee,
>   And nations bow down to thee:
> Be lord over thy brethren,
>   And let thy mother's sons bow down to thee:
> Cursed be every one that curseth thee,
>   And blessed be every one that blesseth thee.

And it came to pass, as soon as Isaac had made an end of blessing Jacob, and Jacob was yet scarce gone out from the presence of Isaac his father, that Esau his brother came in from his hunting. And he also made savoury meat, and brought it unto his father; and he said unto his father, Let my father arise, and eat of his son's venison, that thy soul may bless me. And Isaac his father said unto him, Who art thou? And he said, I am thy son, thy firstborn, Esau. And Isaac trembled very exceedingly, and said, Who then is he that hath taken venison, and brought it me, and I have eaten of all before thou camest, and have blessed him? yea, and he shall be blessed. When Esau heard the words of his father, he cried with an exceeding great and bitter cry, and said unto his father, Bless me, even me also, O my father. And he said, Thy brother came with guile, and hath taken away thy blessing. And he said, Is not he rightly named 'Jacob'? for he hath 'supplanted' me these two times: he took away my birthright; and, behold, now he hath taken away my blessing. And he said, Hast thou not reserved a blessing for me? And Isaac answered and said unto Esau, Behold, I have made him thy lord, and all his brethren have I given to him for servants; and with corn and wine have I sustained him: and what then shall I do for thee, my son? And Esau said unto his father, Hast thou but one blessing, my father? bless me, even me also, O my father. And Esau lifted up his voice, and wept. And Isaac his father answered and said unto him:

Behold, away from the fatness of the earth shall be thy
    dwelling,
And away from the dew of heaven from above;
    And by thy sword thou shalt live:
And thou shalt serve thy brother;
And it shall come to pass when thou shalt break loose,
    That thou shalt shake his yoke from off thy neck.

And Esau hated Jacob because of the blessing wherewith his father blessed him: and Esau said in his heart, The days of mourning for my father are at hand; then will I slay my brother Jacob. And the words of Esau her elder son were told to Rebekah; and she sent and called Jacob her younger son, and said unto him, Behold thy brother Esau, as touching thee, doth comfort himself, purposing to kill thee. Now therefore, my son, obey my voice; and arise, flee thou to Laban my brother to Haran; and tarry with him a few days, until thy brother's fury turn away; until thy brother's anger turn away from thee, and he forget that which thou hast done to him: then I will send, and fetch thee from thence: why should I be bereaved of you both in one day?

And Jacob went out from Beer-sheba, and went toward Haran. And he lighted upon a certain place, and tarried there all night, because the sun was set; and he took one of the stones of the place, and put it under his head, and lay down in that place to sleep. And he dreamed, and behold a ladder set up on the earth, and the top of it reached to heaven: and behold the angels of God ascending and descending on it. And, behold, the LORD stood above it, and said, I am the LORD the God of Abraham thy father, and the God of Isaac: the land whereon thou liest, to thee will I give it, and to thy seed; and thy seed shall be as the dust of the earth, and thou shalt spread abroad to the west, and to the east, and to the north, and to the south: and in thee and in thy seed shall all the families of the earth be blessed. And, behold, I am with thee, and will keep thee whithersoever thou goest, and will bring thee again into this land; for I will not leave thee, until I have done that which I have spoken to thee of. And Jacob awaked out of his sleep, and he said, Surely the LORD is in this place; and I knew it not. And he was afraid, and said, How dreadful is this place! this is none other but the house of God, and this is the gate of heaven. And Jacob rose up early in the morning, and took the stone that he had put under his head, and set it up for a pillar, and poured oil upon the top of it. And he called the name of that place Beth-el. And Jacob vowed a vow, saying, If God will be with me, and will keep me in this way that I go, and will give me bread to eat, and raiment to put on, so that I come again to my father's house in peace, then shall the LORD be my God, and this stone, which I have set up for a pillar, shall be God's house: and of all that thou shalt give me I will surely give the tenth unto thee.

ix

Joseph and his Brethren

Joseph and his Brethren in Canaan

Joseph, being seventeen years old, was feeding the flock with his brethren; and Joseph brought the evil report of them unto their father. Now Israel loved Joseph more than all his children, because he was the son of his old age: and he made him a coat of many colours. And his brethren saw that their father loved him more than all his brethren; and they hated him, and could not speak peaceably unto him. And Joseph dreamed a dream, and he told it to his brethren: and they hated him yet the more. And he said unto them, Hear, I pray you, this dream which

I have dreamed: for, behold, we were binding sheaves in the field, and, lo, my sheaf arose, and also stood upright; and, behold, your sheaves came round about, and made obeisance to my sheaf. And his brethren said to him, Shalt thou indeed reign over us? or shalt thou indeed have dominion over us? And they hated him yet the more for his dreams, and for his words. And he dreamed yet another dream, and told it to his brethren, and said, Behold, I have dreamed yet a dream; and, behold, the sun and the moon and eleven stars made obeisance to me. And he told it to his father, and to his brethren; and his father rebuked him, and said unto him, What is this dream that thou hast dreamed? Shall I and thy mother and thy brethren indeed come to bow down ourselves to thee to the earth? And his brethren envied him; but his father kept the saying in mind.

And his brethren went to feed their father's flock in Shechem. And Israel said unto Joseph, Do not thy brethren feed the flock in Shechem? come, and I will send thee unto them. And he said to him, Here am I. And he said to him, Go now, see whether it be well with thy brethren, and well with the flock; and bring me word again. So he sent him out of the vale of Hebron, and he came to Shechem. And a certain man found him, and, behold, he was wandering in a field: and the man asked him, saying, What seekest thou? And he said, I seek my brethren: tell me, I pray thee, where they are feeding the flock.

Genesis ✥   Joseph

And the man said, They are departed hence: for I heard them say, Let us go to Dothan. And Joseph went after his brethren, and found them in Dothan. And they saw him afar off, and before he came near unto them, they conspired against him to slay him. And they said one to another, Behold, this dreamer cometh. Come now therefore, and let us slay him, and cast him into one of the pits, and we will say, An evil beast hath devoured him: and we shall see what will become of his dreams. And Reuben said unto them, Shed no blood; cast him into this pit that is in the wilderness, but lay no hand upon him: that he might deliver him out of their hand, to restore him to his father. And it came to pass, when Joseph was come unto his brethren, that they stript Joseph of his coat, the coat of many colours that was on him; and they took him, and cast him into the pit: and the pit was empty, there was no water in it. And they sat down to eat bread: and they lifted up their eyes and looked, and, behold, a travelling company of Ishmaelites came from Gilead, with their camels bearing spicery and balm and myrrh, going to carry it down to Egypt. And Judah said unto his brethren, What profit is it if we slay our brother and conceal his blood? Come, and let us sell him to the Ishmaelites, and let not our hand be upon him; for he is our brother, our flesh. And his brethren hearkened unto him; and they drew and lifted up Joseph out of the pit, and sold Joseph to the Ishmaelites for twenty pieces of silver. And they brought Joseph into Egypt. And Reuben returned unto the pit; and, behold, Joseph was not in the pit; and he rent his clothes. And he returned unto his brethren, and said, The child is not; and I, whither shall I go? And they took Joseph's coat, and killed a he-goat, and dipped the coat in the blood; and they sent the coat of many colours, and they brought it to their father; and said, This have we found: know now whether it be thy son's coat or not. And he knew it, and said, It is my son's coat; an evil beast hath devoured him; Joseph is without doubt torn in pieces. And Jacob rent his garments, and put sackcloth upon his loins, and mourned for his son many days. And all his sons and all his daughters rose up to comfort him; but he refused to be comforted; and he said, For I will go down to the grave to my son mourning.

Joseph as a Slave in Egypt

And Joseph was brought down to Egypt; and Potiphar, an officer of Pharaoh's, the captain of the guard, an Egyptian, bought him of the hand of the Ishmaelites, which had brought him down thither. And the LORD was with Joseph and he was a prosperous man; and he was in the house of his master the Egyptian. And his master saw that the LORD was with him, and that the LORD made all that he did to prosper in his hand. And Joseph found grace in his sight, and he ministered unto him: and he made him overseer over his house, and all that he had he put into his hand. And it came to pass from the time that he made him overseer in his house, and over all that he had, that the LORD blessed the Egyptian's house for Joseph's sake; and the blessing of the LORD was upon all that he had, in the house and in the field. And he left all that he had in Joseph's hand; and he knew not aught that was with him, save the bread which he did eat.

And Joseph was comely and well favoured. And it came to pass after these things, that his master's wife cast her eyes upon Joseph; and as she spake to Joseph day by day, he hearkened not unto her. And it came to pass about this time, that he went into the house to do his work; and there was none of the men of the house there within. And she caught him by his garment: and he left his garment in her hand, and fled, and got him out. And she laid up his garment by her, until his master came home. And she spake unto him according to these words, saying, The Hebrew servant, which thou hast brought unto us, came in unto me to mock me: and it came to pass, as I lifted up my voice and cried, that he left his garment by me, and fled out. And it came to pass, when his master heard the words of his wife, which she spake unto him, saying, After this manner did thy servant to me; that his wrath was kindled. And Joseph's master took him, and put him into the prison, the place where the king's prisoners were bound: and he was there in the prison. But the LORD was with Joseph, and shewed kindness unto him, and gave him favour in the sight of the keeper of the prison. And the keeper of the prison committed to Joseph's hand all the prisoners that were in the prison; and whatsoever they did there, he was the doer of it. The keeper of the prison looked not to any thing that was under his hand, because the LORD was with him; and that which he did, the LORD made it to prosper.

And it came to pass after these things, that the butler of the king of Egypt and his baker offended their lord the king of Egypt. And Pharaoh was wroth against his two officers, against the chief of the butlers, and against the chief of the bakers. And he put them in ward in the house of the captain of the guard, into the prison, the place where Joseph was bound. And the captain of the guard charged Joseph with them, and he ministered unto them: and they continued a season in ward. And they dreamed a dream both of them, each man his dream, in one night, each man according to the interpretation of his dream, the butler and the baker of the king of Egypt, which were bound in the prison. And Joseph came in unto them in the morning, and saw them, and, behold, they were sad. And he asked Pharaoh's officers that were with him in ward in his master's house, saying, Wherefore look ye so sadly today? And they said unto him, We have dreamed a dream, and there is none that can interpret it. And Joseph said unto them, Do not interpretations belong to God? tell it me, I pray you. And the chief butler told his dream to Joseph, and said to him, In my dream, behold, a vine was before me; and in the vine were three branches: and it was as though it budded, and its blossoms shot forth; and the clusters thereof brought forth ripe grapes: and Pharaoh's cup was in my hand; and I took the grapes, and pressed them into Pharaoh's cup, and I gave the cup into Pharaoh's hand. And Joseph said unto him, This is the interpretation of it: the three branches are three days; within yet three days shall Pharaoh lift up thine head, and restore thee unto thine office: and thou shalt give Pharaoh's cup into his hand, after the former manner when thou wast his butler. But have me in thy remembrance when it shall be well with thee, and shew kindness, I pray thee, unto me, and make mention of me unto Pharaoh, and bring me out of this house: for indeed I was stolen away out of the land of the Hebrews: and here also have I done nothing that they should put me into the dungeon. When the chief baker saw that the interpretation was good, he said unto Joseph, I also was in my dream, and, behold, three baskets of white bread were on my head: and in the uppermost basket there was of all manner of bakemeats for Pharaoh; and the birds did eat them out of the basket upon my head. And Joseph answered and said, This is the interpretation thereof: the three baskets are three days; within yet three days shall Pharaoh lift up thy head from off thee, and shall hang thee on a tree; and the birds shall eat thy flesh from off thee. And it came to pass the third day, which was Pharaoh's birthday, that he made a feast unto all his servants: and he lifted up the head of the chief butler and the head of the chief baker among his servants. And he restored the chief butler unto his butlership again; and he gave the cup into Pharaoh's hand: but he hanged the chief baker: as Joseph had interpreted to them. Yet did not the chief butler remember Joseph, but forgat him.

How in one day Joseph passed from a Slave to a Prime Minister

And it came to pass at the end of two full years, that Pharaoh dreamed: and, behold, he stood by the river. And, behold, there came up out of the river seven kine, well favoured and fatfleshed; and they fed in the reed-grass. And, behold, seven other kine came up after them out of the river, ill favoured and leanfleshed; and stood by the other kine upon the brink of the river. And the ill favoured and leanfleshed kine did eat up the seven well favoured and fat kine. So Pharaoh awoke. And he slept and dreamed a second time: and, behold, seven ears of corn came up upon one stalk, rank and good. And, behold, seven ears, thin and blasted with the east wind, sprung up after them. And the thin ears swallowed up the seven rank and full ears. And Pharaoh awoke, and, behold, it

Genesis &ep; Joseph

was a dream. And it came to pass in the morning that his spirit was troubled; and he sent and called for all the magicians of Egypt, and all the wise men thereof: and Pharaoh told them his dream; but there was none that could interpret them unto Pharaoh. Then spake the chief butler unto Pharaoh, saying, I do remember my faults this day: Pharaoh was wroth with his servants, and put me in ward in the house of the captain of the guard, me and the chief baker: and we dreamed a dream in one night, I and he; we dreamed each man according to the interpretation of his dream. And there was with us there a young man, an Hebrew, servant to the captain of the guard; and we told him, and he interpreted to us our dreams; to each man according to his dream he did interpret. And it came to pass, as he interpreted to us, so it was; me he restored unto mine office, and him he hanged.

Then Pharaoh sent and called Joseph, and they brought him hastily out of the dungeon: and he shaved himself, and changed his raiment, and came in unto Pharaoh. And Pharaoh said unto Joseph, I have dreamed a dream, and there is none that can interpret it: and I have heard say of thee, that when thou hearest a dream thou canst interpret it. And Joseph answered Pharaoh, saying, It is not in me: God shall give Pharaoh an answer of peace. And Pharaoh spake unto Joseph, In my dream, behold, I stood upon the brink of the river: and, behold, there came up out of the river seven kine, fatfleshed and well favoured;

and they fed in the reed-grass: and, behold, seven other kine came up after them, poor and very ill favoured and leanfleshed, such as I never saw in all the land of Egypt for badness: and the lean and ill favoured kine did eat up the first seven fat kine: and when they had eaten them up, it could not be known that they had eaten them; but they were still ill favoured, as at the beginning. So I awoke. And I saw in my dream, and, behold, seven ears came up upon one stalk, full and good: and, behold, seven ears, withered, thin, and blasted with the east wind, sprung up after them: and the thin ears swallowed up the seven good ears: and I told it unto the magicians; but there was none that could declare it to me. And Joseph said unto Pharaoh, The dream of Pharaoh is one: what God is about to do he hath declared unto Pharaoh. The seven good kine are seven years; and the seven good ears are seven years: the dream is one. And the seven lean and ill favoured kine that came up after them are seven years, and also the seven empty ears blasted with the east wind; they shall be seven years of famine. That is the thing which I spake unto Pharaoh: what God is about to do he hath shewed unto Pharaoh. Behold, there come seven years of great plenty throughout all the land of Egypt: and there shall arise after them seven years of famine; and all the plenty shall be forgotten in the land of Egypt; and the famine shall consume the land; and the plenty shall not be known in the land by reason of that

Genesis — Joseph

famine which followeth; for it shall be very grievous. And for that the dream was doubled unto Pharaoh twice, it is because the thing is established by God, and God will shortly bring it to pass. Now therefore let Pharaoh look out a man discreet and wise, and set him over the land of Egypt. Let Pharaoh do this, and let him appoint overseers over the land, and take up the fifth part of the land of Egypt in the seven plenteous years. And let them gather all the food of these good years that come, and lay up corn under the hand of Pharaoh for food in the cities, and let them keep it. And the food shall be for a store to the land against the seven years of famine, which shall be in the land of Egypt; that the land perish not through the famine.

And the thing was good in the eyes of Pharaoh, and in the eyes of all his servants. And Pharaoh said unto his servants, Can we find such a one as this, a man in whom the spirit of God is? And Pharaoh said unto Joseph, Forasmuch as God hath shewed thee all this, there is none so discreet and wise as thou: thou shalt be over my house, and according unto thy word shall all my people be ruled: only in the throne will I be greater than thou. And Pharaoh took off his signet ring from his hand, and put it upon Joseph's hand, and arrayed him in vestures of fine linen, and put a gold chain about his neck; and he made him to ride in the second chariot which he had; and they cried before him, Bow the knee: and he set him over all the land of Egypt.

Joseph and his Brethren in Egypt

And the seven years of plenty, that was in the land of Egypt, came to an end. And the seven years of famine began to come, according as Joseph had said: and there was famine in all lands; but in all the land of Egypt there was bread. And all countries came into Egypt to Joseph for to buy corn; because the famine was sore in all the earth.

Now Jacob saw that there was corn in Egypt, and Jacob said unto his sons, Why do ye look one upon another? And he said, Behold, I have heard that there is corn in Egypt: get you down thither, and buy for us from thence; that we may live, and not die. And Joseph's ten brethren went down to buy corn from Egypt. But Benjamin, Joseph's brother, Jacob sent not with his brethren; for he said, Lest peradventure mischief befall him. And the sons of Israel came to buy among those that came; for the famine was in the land of Canaan. And Joseph was the governor over the land; he it was that sold to all the people of the land: and Joseph's brethren came, and bowed down themselves to him with their faces to the earth. And Joseph saw his brethren, and he knew them, but made himself strange unto them, and spake roughly with them; and he said unto them, Whence come ye? And they said, From the land of Canaan to buy food. And Joseph knew his brethren, but they knew not him. And Joseph remembered the dreams which he dreamed of them, and said unto them, Ye are spies; to see the nakedness of the land ye are come. And they said unto him, Nay, my lord, but to buy food are thy servants come. We are all one man's sons; we are true men, thy servants are no spies. And he said unto them, Nay, but to see the nakedness of the land ye are come. And they said, We thy servants are twelve brethren, the sons of one man in the land of Canaan; and, behold, the youngest is this day with our father, and one is not. And Joseph said unto them, That is it that I spake unto you, saying, Ye are spies: hereby ye shall be proved: by the life of Pharaoh ye shall not go forth hence, except your youngest brother come hither. Send one of you, and let him fetch your brother, and ye shall be bound, that your words may be proved, whether there be truth in you: or else by the life of Pharaoh surely ye are spies. And he put them all together into ward three days.

And Joseph said unto them the third day, This do, and live; for I·fear God: if ye be true men, let one of your brethren be bound in your prison house; but go ye, carry corn for the famine of your houses: and bring your youngest brother unto me; so shall your words be verified, and ye shall not die. And they did so. And they said one to another, We are verily guilty concerning our brother, in that we saw the distress of his soul, when he besought us, and we would not hear; therefore is this distress come upon us. And Reuben answered them, saying, Spake I not unto you, saying, Do not sin against the child; and ye would not hear? therefore also, behold, his blood is required. And they knew not that Joseph understood them; for there was an interpreter between them. And he turned himself about from them, and wept; and he returned to them, and spake to them, and took Simeon from among them, and bound him before their eyes. Then Joseph commanded to fill their vessels with corn, and to restore every man's money into his sack, and to give them provision for the way: and thus was it done unto them. And they laded their asses with their corn, and departed thence. And as one of them opened his sack to give his ass provender in the lodging place, he espied his money; and, behold, it was in the mouth of his sack. And he said unto his brethren, My money is restored; and, lo, it is even in my sack: and their heart failed them, and they turned trembling one to another, saying, What is this that God hath done unto us?

And they came unto Jacob their father unto the land of Canaan, and told him all that had befallen them: saying, The man, the lord of the land, spake roughly with us, and took us for spies of the country. And we said unto him, We are true men; we are no spies: we be twelve brethren, sons of our father; one is not, and the youngest is this day with our father in the land of Canaan. And the man, the lord of the land, said unto us, Hereby shall I know that ye are true men; leave one of your brethren with me and take corn for the famine of your houses, and go your way: and bring your youngest brother unto me: then shall I know that ye are no spies, but that ye are true men: so will I deliver you your brother, and ye shall traffick in the land. And it came to pass as they emptied their sacks, that, behold, every man's bundle of money was in his sack: and when they and their father saw their bundles of money, they were afraid. And Jacob their father said unto them, Me have ye bereaved of my children: Joseph is not, and Simeon is not, and ye will take Benjamin away: all these things are against me. And Reuben spake unto his father, saying, Slay my two sons, if I bring him not to thee: deliver him into my hand, and I will bring him to thee again. And he said, My son shall not go down with you; for his brother is dead, and he only is left: if mischief befall him by the way in the which ye go, then shall ye bring down my gray hairs with sorrow to the grave.

And the famine was sore in the land. And it came to pass, when they had eaten up the corn which they had brought out of Egypt, their father said unto them, Go again, buy us a little food. And Judah spake unto him, saying, The man did solemnly protest unto us, saying, Ye shall not see my face, except your brother be with you. If thou wilt send our brother with us, we will go down and buy thee food: but if thou wilt not send him, we will not go down: for the man said unto us, Ye shall not see my face, except your brother be with you. And Israel said,

Wherefore dealt ye so ill with me, as to tell the man whether ye had yet a brother? And they said, The man asked straitly concerning ourselves, and concerning our kindred, saying, Is your father yet alive? have ye another brother? and we told him according to the tenor of these words: could we in any wise know that he would say, Bring your brother down? And Judah said unto Israel his father, Send the lad with me, and we will arise and go; that we may live, and not die, both we, and thou, and also our little ones. I will be surety for him; of my hand shalt thou require him: if I bring him not unto thee, and set him before thee, then let me bear the blame for ever: for except we had lingered, surely we had now returned a second time. And their father Israel said unto them, If it be so now, do this; take of the choice fruits of the land in your vessels, and carry down the man a present, a little balm, and a little honey, spicery and myrrh, nuts, and almonds: and take double money in your hand; and the money that was returned in the mouth of your sacks carry again in your hand; peradventure it was an oversight: take also your brother, and arise, go again unto the man: and God Almighty give you mercy before the man, that he may release unto you your other brother and Benjamin. And if I be bereaved of my children, I am bereaved.

And the men took that present, and they took double money in their hand, and Benjamin; and rose up, and went down to Egypt, and stood before Joseph. And when

Joseph saw Benjamin with them, he said to the steward of his house, Bring the men into the house, and slay, and make ready; for the men shall dine with me at noon. And the man did as Joseph bade; and the man brought the men into Joseph's house. And the men were afraid, because they were brought into Joseph's house; and they said, Because of the money that was returned in our sacks at the first time are we brought in; that he may seek occasion against us, and fall upon us, and take us for bondmen, and our asses. And they came near to the steward of Joseph's house, and they spake unto him at the door of the house, and said, Oh my lord, we came indeed down at the first time to buy food: and it came to pass, when we came to the lodging place, that we opened our sacks, and, behold, every man's money was in the mouth of his sack, our money in full weight: and we have brought it again in our hand. And other money have we brought down in our hand to buy food: we know not who put our money in our sacks. And he said, Peace be to you, fear not: your God, and the God of your father, hath given you treasure in your sacks: I had your money. And he brought Simeon out unto them. And the man brought the men into Joseph's house, and gave them water, and they washed their feet; and he gave their asses provender.

And they made ready the present against Joseph came at noon: for they heard that they should eat bread there. And when Joseph came home, they brought him the present which was in their hand into the house, and bowed down themselves to him to the earth. And he asked them of their welfare, and said, Is your father well, the old man of whom ye spake? Is he yet alive? And they said, Thy servant our father is well, he is yet alive. And they bowed the head, and made obeisance. And he lifted up his eyes, and saw Benjamin his brother, his mother's son, and said, Is this your youngest brother, of whom ye spake unto me? And he said, God be gracious unto thee, my son. And Joseph made haste; and he sought where to weep; and he entered into his chamber, and wept there. And he washed his face, and came out; and he refrained himself, and said, Set on bread. And they set on for him by himself, and for them by themselves, and for the Egyptians, which did eat with him, by themselves: because the Egyptians might not eat bread with the Hebrews; for that is an abomination unto the Egyptians. And they sat before him, the firstborn according to his birthright, and the youngest according to his youth: and the men marvelled one with another. And he took and sent messes unto them from before him: but Benjamin's mess was five times so much as any of theirs. And they drank and were merry with him.

And he commanded the steward of his house, saying, Fill the men's sacks with food, as much as they can carry, and put every man's money in his sack's mouth. And put my cup, the silver cup, in the sack's mouth of the youngest, and his corn money. And he did according to the word that Joseph had spoken. As soon as the morning was light, the men were sent away, they and their asses. And when they were gone out of the city, and were not yet far off, Joseph said unto his steward, Up, follow after the men; and when thou dost overtake them, say unto them, Wherefore have ye rewarded evil for good? Is not this it in which my lord drinketh, and whereby he indeed divineth? ye have done evil in so doing. And he overtook them, and he spake unto them these words. And they said unto him, Wherefore speaketh my lord such words as these? God forbid that thy servants should do such a thing. Behold, the money, which we found in our sacks' mouths, we brought again unto thee out of the land of Canaan: how then should we steal out of thy lord's house silver or gold? With whomsoever of thy servants it be found, let him die, and we also will be my lord's bondmen. And he said, Now also let it be according unto your words: he with whom it is found shall be my bondman; and ye shall be blameless. Then they hasted, and took down every man his sack to the ground, and opened every man his sack. And he searched, and began at the eldest, and left at the youngest: and the cup was found in Benjamin's sack. Then they rent their clothes, and laded every man his ass, and returned to the city.

And Judah and his brethren came to Joseph's house; and he was yet there: and they fell before him on the ground. And Joseph said unto them, What deed is this that ye have done? know ye not that such a man as I can indeed divine? And Judah said, What shall we say unto my lord? what shall we speak? or how shall we clear ourselves? God hath found out the iniquity of thy servants: behold, we are my lord's bondmen, both we, and he also in whose hand the cup is found. And he said, God forbid that I should do so: the man in whose hand the cup is found, he shall be my bondman; but as for you, get you up in peace unto your father.

Then Judah came near unto him, and said, Oh my lord, let thy servant, I pray thee, speak a word in my lord's ears, and let not thine anger burn against thy servant: for thou art even as Pharaoh. My lord asked his servants, saying, Have ye a father, or a brother? And we said unto my lord, We have a father, an old man, and a child of his old age, a little one; and his brother is dead, and he alone is left of his mother, and his father loveth him. And thou saidst unto thy servants, Bring him down unto me, that I may set mine eyes upon him. And we said unto my lord, The lad cannot leave his father: for if he should leave his father, his father would die. And thou saidst unto thy servants, Except your youngest brother come down with you, ye shall see my face no more. And it came to pass when we came up unto thy servant my father, we told him the words of my lord. And our father said, Go again, buy us a little food. And we said, We cannot go down: if our youngest brother be with us, then will we go down: for we may not see the man's face, except our youngest brother be with us. And thy servant my father said unto us, Ye know that my wife bare me two sons: and the one went out from me, and I said, Surely he is torn in pieces; and I have not seen him since: and if he take this one also from me, and mischief befall him, ye shall bring down my gray hairs with sorrow to the grave. Now therefore when I come to thy servant my father, and the lad be not with us; seeing that his life is bound up in the lad's life; it shall come to pass, when he seeth that the lad is not with us, that he will die: and thy servants shall bring down the gray hairs of thy servant our father with sorrow to the grave. For thy servant became surety for the lad unto my father, saying, If I bring him not unto thee, then shall I bear the blame to my father for ever. Now therefore, let thy servant, I pray thee, abide instead of the lad a bondman to my lord; and let the lad go up with his brethren. For how shall I go up to my father, and the lad be not with me? lest I see the evil that shall come on my father.

Then Joseph could not refrain himself before all them that stood by him; and he cried, Cause every man to go out from me. And there stood no man with him, while Joseph made himself known unto his brethren. And he wept aloud: and the Egyptians heard, and the house of Pharaoh heard. And Joseph said unto his brethren, I am

Joseph; doth my father yet live? And his brethren could not answer him; for they were troubled at his presence. And Joseph said unto his brethren, Come near to me, I pray you. And they came near. And he said, I am Joseph your brother whom ye sold into Egypt. And now be not grieved, nor angry with yourselves, that ye sold me hither: for God did send me before you to preserve life. For these two years hath the famine been in the land: and there are yet five years in the which there shall be neither plowing nor harvest. And God sent me before you to preserve you a remnant in the earth, and to save you alive by a great deliverance. So now it was not you that sent me hither, but God: and he hath made me a father to Pharaoh, and lord of all his house, and ruler over all the land of Egypt. Haste ye, and go up to my father, and say unto him, Thus saith thy son Joseph, God hath made me lord of all Egypt: come down unto me, tarry not: and thou shalt dwell in the land of Goshen, and thou shalt be near unto me, thou, and thy children, and thy children's children, and thy flocks, and thy herds, and all that thou hast: and there will I nourish thee; for there are yet five years of famine; lest thou come to poverty, thou, and thy household, and all that thou hast. And, behold, your eyes see, and the eyes of my brother Benjamin, that it is my mouth that speaketh unto you. And ye shall tell my father of all my glory in Egypt, and of all that ye have seen; and ye shall haste and bring down my father hither. And he fell upon his brother Benjamin's neck, and wept; and Benjamin wept upon his neck. And he kissed all his brethren, and wept upon them: and after that his brethren talked with him.

And the fame thereof was heard in Pharaoh's house, saying, Joseph's brethren are come: and it pleased Pharaoh well, and his servants. And Pharaoh said unto Joseph, Say unto thy brethren, This do ye; lade your beasts, and go, get you into the land of Canaan; and take your father and your households, and come unto me: and I will give you the good of the land of Egypt, and ye shall eat the fat of the land. Now thou art commanded, this do ye; take you wagons, out of the land of Egypt for your little ones, and for your wives, and bring your father, and come. Also regard not your stuff; for the good of all the land of Egypt is yours. And the sons of Israel did so: and Joseph gave them wagons according to the commandment of Pharaoh, and gave them provision for the way. To all of them he gave each man changes of raiment; but to Benjamin he gave three hundred pieces of silver, and five changes of raiment. And to his father he sent after this manner; ten asses laden with the good things of Egypt, and ten she-asses, laden with corn and bread and victual for his father by the way. So he sent his brethren away, and they departed: and he said unto them, See that ye fall not out by the way.

Joseph   Bible Stories

Journey of the Children of Israel into Egypt

And they went up out of Egypt, and came into the land of Canaan unto Jacob their father. And they told him, saying, Joseph is yet alive, and he is ruler over all the land of Egypt. And his heart fainted, for he believed them not. And they told him all the words of Joseph, which he had said unto them: and when he saw the wagons which Joseph had sent to carry him, the spirit of Jacob their father revived: and Israel said, It is enough; Joseph my son is yet alive: I will go and see him before I die.

And Israel took his journey with all that he had, and came to Beer-sheba, and offered sacrifices unto the God of his father Isaac. And God spake unto Israel in the visions of the night, and said, Jacob, Jacob. And he said, Here am I. And he said, I am God, the God of thy father: fear not to go down into Egypt; for I will there make of thee a great nation: I will go down with thee into Egypt; and I will also surely bring thee up again: and Joseph shall put his hand upon thine eyes. And Jacob rose up from Beer-sheba: and the sons of Israel carried Jacob their father, and their little ones, and their wives, in the wagons which Pharaoh had sent to carry him. And they took their cattle, and their goods, which they had gotten in the land of Canaan, and came into Egypt, Jacob, and all his seed with him: his sons, and his sons' sons with him, his daughters, and his sons' daughters, and all his seed brought he with him into Egypt.

And he sent Judah before him unto Joseph, to shew the way before him unto Goshen; and they came into the land of Goshen. And Joseph made ready his chariot, and went up to meet Israel his father, to Goshen; and he presented himself unto him, and fell on his neck, and wept on his neck a good while. And Israel said unto Joseph, Now let me die, since I have seen thy face, that thou art yet alive.

Then Joseph went in and told Pharaoh, and said, My father and my brethren, and their flocks, and their herds, and all that they have, are come out of the land of Canaan; and, behold, they are in the land of Goshen. And from among his brethren he took five men, and presented them unto Pharaoh. And Pharaoh said unto his brethren, What is your occupation? And they said unto Pharaoh, Thy servants are shepherds, both we, and our fathers. And they said unto Pharaoh, To sojourn in the land are we come; for there is no pasture for thy servants' flocks; for the famine is sore in the land of Canaan: now therefore, we pray thee, let thy servants dwell in the land of Goshen. And Pharaoh spake unto Joseph, saying, Thy father and thy brethren are come unto thee: the land of Egypt is before thee; in the best of the land make thy father and thy brethren to dwell: in the land of Goshen let them dwell: and if thou knowest any able men among them, then make them rulers over my cattle. And Joseph brought in Jacob his father, and set him before Pharaoh: and Jacob blessed Pharaoh. And Pharaoh said unto Jacob, How many are the days of the years of thy life? And Jacob said unto Pharaoh, The days of the years of my pilgrimage are an hundred and thirty years: few and evil have been the days of the years of my life, and they have not attained unto the days of the years of the life of my fathers in the days of their pilgrimage. And Jacob blessed Pharaoh, and went out from the presence of Pharaoh. And Joseph placed his father and his brethren, and gave them a possession in the land of Egypt, in the best of the land, as Pharaoh had commanded. And Joseph nourished his father, and his brethren, and all his father's household, with bread, according to their families.

Genesis

Notes to Genesis

i. This story of the Creation differs from other Bible stories. It reads like a chant, with refrains repeated, one at the beginning and one at the end of each 'day'; thus:

{ *And God said—*
  [Creation of Light]
And there was evening and there was morning, one day

{ *And God said—*
  [Creation of the Firmament dividing waters from waters]
And there was evening and there was morning, a second day

{ *And God said—*
  [Creation of Land]
  And God said—
  [Creation of Vegetation, Climax of inanimate Nature]
And there was evening and there was morning, a third day

{ *And God said—*
  [Creation of Lights]
And there was evening and there was morning, a fourth day

{ *And God said—*
  [Creation of Life in the Firmament and in the waters]
And there was evening and there was morning, a fifth day

{ *And God said—*
  [Creation of Life on Land]
  And God said—
  [Creation of Man, Climax of animate Nature]
And there was evening and there was morning, the sixth day

Notes → **Bible Stories**

A glance at the above scheme shows how the creation thus described falls into two similar parts, the first day corresponding with the fourth, the second with the fifth, the third with the sixth. The impression left upon our minds is (1) that the whole universe is one harmonious plan, (2) that each portion of this universe is God's own work. — The closing paragraph, with its six days of work and one of rest, brings out the great law of life which we call the week. — *A firmament . . . let it divide the waters from the waters.* The word *firmament* means *barrier:* the rain clouds [*waters above the firmament*] float upon the expanse of air, the seas and rivers [*waters under the firmament*] are below it.

ii. This incident of the Temptation in the Garden of Eden, unlike most Scripture stories, is told only in brief outline. It is a good exercise to study the expansion of it into a vivid picture in the ninth book of Milton's *Paradise Lost.* — *The Cherubim* (plural): one of the orders of Angels is called by this name.

iii. *Unto thee is its desire, but thou shouldest rule over it:* the words are an allusion to what was spoken in ii to the woman: *Thy desire shall be to thy husband, and he shall rule over thee.* Sin (so to speak) comes coaxing, like a false wife: but Cain must be the master over his passions.

iv. *Thirty cubits:* the word means the bend of the arm; the Hebrew unit of length was from the elbow to the wrist of the average man. — *Fountains of the great deep . . . windows of heaven:* these are poetical expressions to describe the *waters under* and *waters above the firmament* (see note on i). — *The mountains of Ararat:* a mountain region in what is now Armenia.

Genesis   Notes

v. Canaan (or Palestine) lies along the west coast of Asia; Haran is supposed to be in the far east, between the great rivers Tigris and Euphrates. — *Abram* is 'lofty father'; *Abraham*, 'father of a multitude of nations.'

vi. '*Isaac*' . . . '*laugh*': it will be understood that throughout this volume this use of inverted commas implies that the pair of words so indicated have a resemblance of sound in the original language.

vii. *Mesopotamia*: the word means *between the rivers*; it is applied to the land that lies between the great rivers Tigris and Euphrates, the region from which originally Abraham came. — *My master's brother's daughter*: the word *daughter* is here used for *descendant*. In reality she was a grand-daughter.

viii. This story, like some others in Scripture, is a combination of prose and verse: the verse being reserved for the words of blessing, or other prophetic speeches. In Biblical poetry, verse is not constituted by rhyme, or by a particular number of syllables in each line, but by 'parallelism': that is, the two (or three) lines of a set are found to run parallel in their clauses. Thus, if Jacob had spoken in prose he would have said: *Let peoples serve thee; be lord over thy brethren; cursed be every one that curseth thee.* When instead of this he says,

> *Let peoples serve thee,*
>   *And nations bow down to thee,*
> *Be lord over thy brethren,*
>   *And let thy mother's sons bow down to thee;*
> *Cursed be every one that curseth thee,*
>   *And blessed be every one that blesseth thee —*

the addition to each clause of a new clause parallel with it leaves on the ear the effect of rhythm: which makes verse. For a more precise account of the metrical system of this poetry, see the *Biblical Masterpieces* volume of this series, page 241. — *Beth-el* means house of God. — All the parties to this story are in the wrong. Isaac abuses his patriarchal authority by seeking to limit the succession of the Chosen People to a favourite son; Rebekah plans a trick by which he is made to give the blessing of the succession to the son for whom he did not intend it; Jacob lends himself to this trick. Esau, innocent in this incident, had been in the wrong by his whole style of living: he was an ancestor and type of mountain peoples, living a hunter's life: they are fiery and impulsive, but easily appeased. In one of his sudden impulses (referred to on page 32), Esau had sold to Jacob his rights as elder son, in return for a savoury soup which Jacob was cooking when Esau returned hungry from a hunt. Such a character excludes from the great nations who carry on the history of the world. Jacob, with all his faults, has capacity for growth, and it is in his line that the succession of the Chosen People is continued. Thus the wrong actions of all four are overruled for good.

ix. This is one of the most beautiful stories in all literature. (1) It has an important place in history, Joseph being a link between the Children of Israel and the empire of Egypt. (2) Note the character of Joseph, how he makes an impression on all with whom he comes into contact. (3) Note also the sketches of varied life which make a background to the story as it moves along — such as glimpses of wandering shepherd life,

Genesis — Notes

trading caravans, palace life in Egypt. (4) There is the interest of dreams, five in all, mysterious foretellings which gradually become clear as they are fulfilled. (5) At last we have a double, or, as it is called, 'ironic' situation, when Joseph recognises his brethren but is not recognised by them. This situation of affairs, when it has once arisen, is prolonged to the utmost length by Joseph's conflict of feelings, between resentment and family affection. A climax is found when, among the very men who once united to enslave their brother Joseph, one is now found consenting to be a slave in order to deliver their brother Benjamin. (6) Beyond all other interests there is that of the providential overruling of human events: see page 56. — *Is not this it . . . whereby he divineth?* It must be remembered that Joseph is still supposed to be an Egyptian lord. The Egyptians believed much in magic, and *divination* (of the future) was part of this: images of idols were no doubt carved about the cup such as would be used in magical arts.

BIBLE STORIES

THE EXODUS

INTRODUCTION TO THE EXODUS

The second portion of the Bible history is called The Exodus, that is, the Emigration of the Israelites, from Egypt to their promised land of Canaan. This is also the period in which they ceased to be merely a large family, and were formed into a nation, with laws and institutions of their own. Accordingly, in the Bible itself this period is very hard reading, for the history is mostly made up of laws and regulations and figures. But there are three famous stories belonging to the history of The Exodus, and these throw a bright light upon three stages in the growth of Israel.

The first is the story of Moses and the Plagues of Egypt. Egypt is a land of plentiful food and lazy life: the children of Israel yielded to these influences, and gradually lost their manliness. At last they were made slaves by the Egyptians and cruelly persecuted. Moses was raised up to deliver them; and in the narrative of wonders which accompanied their escape from Egypt, we have a picture of the Israelites as they were before the emigration began — a horde of timid and persecuted slaves.

The Bible narrative then tells of their march through the wilderness: how a cloud by day and a fiery cloud by

Introduction — Bible Stories

night led the way, how 'manna,' or bread falling from heaven, fed them, and water flowed from solid rock to give them drink. When mount Sinai was reached we have a second story: how the Law of the Ten Commandments was given amid thunder and lightning by the voice of God. This is the beginning of the long series of laws and regulations for the government of the people, made known from God through Moses.

Then, at great length, the Bible tells of the wandering for forty years in the wilderness, until the generation of Israelites who had been corrupted by life in Egypt had died out, and a new generation was hardened by the rough life of the wilderness, and ready to conquer the promised land. With the history itself are found minute laws and regulations. Just before the end of the history, our third story comes: the famous story of Balaam. This Balaam was a prophet, brought by the enemies of Israel to curse them: by divine inspiration, instead of a curse he uttered blessings. In the words of Balaam's blessings we see Israel, no longer slavish and timid, but a brave and splendidly ordered people, winning the admiration of their enemies.

STORIES FROM THE EXODUS

i. Moses and the Plagues of Egypt
   The Wonderful Preservation of Moses as a Babe
   The Ten Plagues of Egypt
   Overthrow of the Egyptians at the Red Sea
   Song of Moses and Miriam
ii. Law of the Ten Commandments from Sinai
iii. The Witness of Balaam to Israel

i

Moses and the Plagues of Egypt

The Wonderful Preservation of Moses as a Babe

Now there arose a new king over Egypt, which knew not Joseph. And he said unto his people, Behold, the people of the children of Israel are more and mightier than we: come, let us deal wisely with them; lest they multiply, and it come to pass, that, when there falleth out any war, they also join themselves unto our enemies, and fight against us, and get them up out of the land. Therefore they did set over them taskmasters to afflict them with their burdens. But the more they afflicted them, the more they multiplied and the more they spread abroad. And Pharaoh charged all his people, saying, Every son that is born ye shall cast into the river, and every daughter ye shall save alive.

And there went a man of the house of Levi, and took to wife a daughter of Levi. And the woman bare a son: and when she saw him that he was a goodly child, she hid him three months. And when she could not longer hide him, she took for him an ark of bulrushes, and daubed it with slime and with pitch; and she put the child therein, and laid it in the flags by the river's brink. And his sister stood afar off, to know what would be done to him. And the daughter of Pharaoh came down to bathe at the river; and her maidens walked along by the river side; and she saw the ark among the flags, and sent her handmaid to fetch it. And she opened it, and saw the child: and, behold, the babe wept. And she had compassion on him, and said, This is one of the Hebrews' children. Then said his sister to Pharaoh's daughter, Shall I go and call thee a nurse of the Hebrew women, that she may nurse the child for thee? And Pharaoh's daughter said to her, Go. And the maid went and called the child's mother. And Pharaoh's daughter said unto her, Take this child away, and nurse it for me, and I will give thee thy wages. And the woman took the child, and nursed it. And the child grew, and she brought him unto Pharaoh's daughter, and he became her son. And she called his name Moses.

The Ten Plagues of Egypt

And Moses was fourscore years old, and Aaron fourscore and three years old, when they spake unto Pharaoh. And the LORD spake unto Moses and unto Aaron, saying, When Pharaoh shall speak unto you, saying, Shew a wonder for you: then thou shalt say unto Aaron, Take thy rod, and cast it down before Pharaoh, that it become a serpent. And Moses and Aaron went in unto Pharaoh, and they did so, as the LORD had commanded: and Aaron cast down his rod before Pharaoh and before his servants, and it became a serpent. Then Pharaoh also called for the wise men and the sorcerers: and they also, the magicians of Egypt, did in like manner with their enchantments. For they cast down every man his rod, and they became serpents: but Aaron's rod swallowed up their rods. And Pharaoh's heart was hardened, and he hearkened not unto them.

And the LORD said unto Moses, Pharaoh's heart is stubborn, he refuseth to let the people go. Get thee unto Pharaoh in the morning: lo, he goeth out unto the water; and thou shalt stand by the river's brink to meet him; and the rod which was turned to a serpent shalt thou take in thine hand. And thou shalt say unto him, The LORD, the God of the Hebrews, hath sent me unto thee, saying, Let my people go, that they may serve me in the wilderness: and, behold, hitherto thou hast not hearkened. Thus saith the LORD, In this thou shalt know that I am the LORD: behold, I will smite with the rod that is in mine hand upon the waters which are in the river, and they shall be turned to blood. And the fish that is in the river shall die, and the river shall stink; and the Egyptians shall loathe to drink water from the river. And the LORD said unto Moses, Say unto Aaron, Take thy rod, and stretch out thine hand over the waters of Egypt, over their rivers, over their streams, and over their pools, and over all their ponds of water, that they may become blood; and there shall be blood throughout all the land of Egypt, both in vessels of wood and in vessels of stone. And Moses and Aaron did so, as the LORD commanded; and he lifted up the rod, and smote the waters that were in the river, in the sight of Pharaoh, and in the sight of his servants; and all the waters that were in the river were turned to blood. And the fish that was in the river died; and the river stank, and the Egyptians could not drink water from the river; and the blood was throughout all the land of Egypt. And the magicians of Egypt did in like manner with their enchantments: and Pharaoh's heart was hardened, and he hearkened not unto them. And Pharaoh turned and went into his house, neither did he lay even this to heart. And all the Egyptians digged round about the river for water to drink; for they could not drink of the water of the river. And seven days were fulfilled, after that the LORD had smitten the river.

And the LORD spake unto Moses, Go in unto Pharaoh, and say unto him, Thus saith the LORD, Let my people go, that they may serve me. And if thou refuse to let them go, behold, I will smite all thy borders with frogs: and the river shall swarm with frogs, which shall go up and come into thine house, and into thy bedchamber, and upon thy bed, and into the house of thy servants, and upon thy people, and into thine ovens, and into thy kneadingtroughs: and the frogs shall come up both upon thee, and upon thy people, and upon all thy servants. And the LORD said unto Moses, Say unto Aaron, Stretch forth thine hand with thy rod over the rivers, over the streams, and over the pools, and cause frogs to come up upon the land of Egypt. And Aaron stretched out his hand over the waters of Egypt: and the frogs came up, and covered the land of Egypt. And the magicians did in like manner with their enchantments, and brought up frogs upon the land of Egypt. Then Pharaoh called for Moses and Aaron, and said, Intreat the LORD, that he take away the frogs from me, and from my people; and I will let the people go, that they may sacrifice unto the LORD. And Moses said unto Pharaoh, Have thou this glory over me: against what time shall I intreat for thee, and for thy servants, and for thy people, that the frogs be destroyed from thee and thy houses, and remain in the river only? And he said, Against tomorrow. And he said, Be it according to thy word: that thou mayest know that there is none like unto the LORD our God. And the frogs shall depart from thee, and from thy houses, and from thy servants, and from thy people; they shall remain in the river only. And Moses and Aaron went out from Pharaoh: and Moses cried unto the LORD concerning the frogs which he had brought upon Pharaoh. And the LORD did according to the word of Moses; and the frogs died out of the houses, out of the courts, and out of the fields. And they gathered them together in heaps: and the land stank. But when Pharaoh saw that there was respite, he hardened his heart, and hearkened not unto them.

And the LORD said unto Moses, Say unto Aaron, Stretch out thy rod, and smite the dust of the earth, that it may become lice throughout all the land of Egypt. And they did so; and Aaron stretched out his hand with his rod, and smote the dust of the earth, and there were lice upon man, and upon beast; all the dust of the earth became lice throughout all the land of Egypt. And the magicians did so with their enchantments to bring forth lice, but they could not: and there were lice upon man, and upon beast. Then the magicians said unto Pharaoh, This is the finger of God: and Pharaoh's heart was hardened, and he hearkened not unto them.

And the LORD said unto Moses, Rise up early in the morning, and stand before Pharaoh; lo, he cometh forth to the water; and say unto him, Thus saith the LORD, Let my people go, that they may serve me. Else, if thou wilt not let my people go, behold, I will send swarms of flies upon thee, and upon thy servants, and upon thy people, and into thy houses: and the houses of the Egyptians shall be full of swarms of flies, and also the ground whereon they are. And I will sever in that day the land of Goshen, in which my people dwell, that no swarms of flies shall be there; to the end thou mayest know that I am the LORD in the midst of the earth. And I will put a division between my people and thy people: by tomorrow shall this sign be. And the LORD did so; and there came grievous swarms of flies into the house of Pharaoh, and into his servants' houses: and in all the land of Egypt the land was corrupted by reason of the swarms of flies. And Pharaoh called for Moses and for Aaron, and said, Go ye, sacrifice to your God in the land. And Moses said, It is not meet so to do; for we shall sacrifice the abomination of the Egyptians to the LORD our God: lo, shall we sacrifice the abomination of the Egyptians before their eyes, and will they not stone us? We will go three days' journey into the wilderness, and sacrifice to the LORD our God, as he shall command us. And Pharaoh said, I will let you go, that ye may sacrifice to the LORD your God in the wilderness; only ye shall not go very far away: intreat for me. And Moses said, Behold, I go out from thee, and I will intreat the LORD that the swarms of flies may depart from Pharaoh, from his servants, and from his people, tomorrow: only let not Pharaoh deal deceitfully any more in not letting the people go to sacrifice to the LORD. And Moses went out from Pharaoh, and intreated the LORD. And the LORD did according to the word of Moses; and he removed the swarms of flies from Pharaoh, from his servants, and from his people; there remained not one. And Pharaoh hardened his heart this time also, and he did not let the people go.

Then the LORD said unto Moses, Go in unto Pharaoh,

and tell him, Thus saith the LORD, the God of the Hebrews, Let my people go, that they may serve me. For if thou refuse to let them go, and wilt hold them still, behold, the hand of the LORD is upon thy cattle which is in the field, upon the horses, upon the asses, upon the camels, upon the herds, and upon the flocks: there shall be a very grievous murrain. And the LORD shall sever between the cattle of Israel and the cattle of Egypt: and there shall nothing die of all that belongeth to the children of Israel. And the LORD appointed a set time, saying, Tomorrow the LORD shall do this thing in the land. And the LORD did that thing on the morrow, and all the cattle of Egypt died: but of the cattle of the children of Israel died not one. And Pharaoh sent, and, behold, there was not so much as one of the cattle of the Israelites dead. But the heart of Pharaoh was stubborn, and he did not let the people go.

And the LORD said unto Moses and unto Aaron, Take to you handfuls of ashes of the furnace, and let Moses sprinkle it toward the heaven in the sight of Pharaoh. And it shall become small dust over all the land of Egypt, and shall be a boil breaking forth with blains upon man and upon beast, throughout all the land of Egypt. And they took ashes of the furnace, and stood before Pharaoh; and Moses sprinkled it up toward heaven; and it became a boil breaking forth with blains upon man and upon beast. And the magicians could not stand before Moses because of the boils; for the boils were upon the magicians, and upon all the Egyptians. And the LORD hardened the heart of Pharaoh, and he hearkened not unto them; as the LORD had spoken unto Moses.

And the LORD said unto Moses, Rise up early in the morning, and stand before Pharaoh, and say unto him, Thus saith the LORD, the God of the Hebrews, Let my people go, that they may serve me. For I will this time send all my plagues upon thine heart, and upon thy servants, and upon thy people; that thou mayest know that there is none like me in all the earth. For now I had put forth my hand, and smitten thee and thy people with pestilence, and thou hadst been cut off from the earth: but in very deed for this cause have I made thee to stand, for to shew thee my power, and that my name may be declared throughout all the earth. As yet exaltest thou thyself against my people, that thou wilt not let them go? Behold, tomorrow about this time I will cause it to rain a very grievous hail, such as hath not been in Egypt since the day it was founded even until now. Now therefore send, hasten in thy cattle and all that thou hast in the field; for every man and beast which shall be found in the field, and shall not be brought home, the hail shall come down upon them, and they shall die. He that feared the word of the LORD among the servants of Pharaoh made his servants and his cattle flee into the houses: and he that regarded not the word of the LORD left his servants and his cattle in the field.

And the LORD said unto Moses, Stretch forth thine hand toward heaven, that there may be hail in all the land of Egypt, upon man, and upon beast, and upon every herb of the field, throughout the land of Egypt. And Moses stretched forth his rod toward heaven: and the LORD sent thunder and hail, and fire ran down unto the earth; and the LORD rained hail upon the land of Egypt. So there was hail, and fire mingled with the hail, very grievous, such as had not been in all the land of Egypt since it became a nation. And the hail smote throughout all the land of Egypt all that was in the field, both man and beast; and the hail smote every herb of the field, and brake every tree of the field. Only in the land of Goshen, where the children of Israel were, was there no hail. And Pharaoh sent, and called for Moses and Aaron, and said unto them, I have sinned this time: the LORD is righteous, and I and my people are wicked. Intreat the LORD; for there hath been enough of these mighty thunderings and hail; and I will let you go, and ye shall stay no longer. And Moses said unto him, As soon as I am gone out of the city, I will spread abroad my hands unto the LORD; the thunders shall cease, neither shall there be any more hail; that thou mayest know that the earth is the LORD's. But as for thee and thy servants, I know that ye will not yet fear the LORD God. And Moses went out of the city from Pharaoh, and spread abroad his hands unto the LORD: and the thunders and hail ceased, and the rain was not poured upon the earth. And when Pharaoh saw that the rain and the hail and the thunders were ceased, he sinned yet more, and hardened his heart, he and his servants. And the heart of Pharaoh was hardened, and he did not let the children of Israel go; as the LORD had spoken by Moses.

And the LORD said unto Moses, Go in unto Pharaoh: for I have hardened his heart, and the heart of his servants, that I might shew these my signs in the midst of them: and that thou mayest tell in the ears of thy son, and of thy son's son, what things I have wrought upon Egypt, and my signs which I have done among them; that ye may know that I am the LORD. And Moses and Aaron went in unto Pharaoh, and said unto him, Thus saith the LORD, the God of the Hebrews, How long wilt thou refuse to humble thyself before me? let my people go, that they may serve me. Else, if thou refuse to let my people go, behold, tomorrow will I bring locusts into thy border: and they shall cover the face of the earth, that one shall not be able to see the earth: and they shall eat the residue of that which is escaped, which remaineth unto you from the hail, and shall eat every tree which groweth for you out of the field: and thy houses shall be filled, and the houses of all thy servants, and the houses of all the Egyptians; as neither thy fathers nor thy fathers' fathers have seen, since the day that they were upon the earth unto this day. And he turned, and went out from Pharaoh.

And Pharaoh's servants said unto him, How long shall this man be a snare unto us? let the men go, that they may serve the LORD their God: knowest thou not yet that Egypt is destroyed? And Moses and Aaron were brought again unto Pharaoh: and he said unto them, Go, serve the LORD your God: but who are they that shall go? And Moses said, We will go with our young and with our old, with our sons and with our daughters, with our flocks and with our herds will we go; for we must hold a feast unto the LORD. And he said unto them, So be the LORD with you, as I will let you go, and your little ones: look to it; for evil is before you. Not so: go now ye that are men, and serve the LORD; for that is what ye desire. And they were driven out from Pharaoh's presence.

And the LORD said unto Moses, Stretch out thine hand over the land of Egypt for the locusts, that they may come up upon the land of Egypt, and eat every herb of the land, even all that the hail hath left. And Moses stretched forth his rod over the land of Egypt, and the LORD brought an east wind upon the land all that day, and all the night; and when it was morning, the east wind brought the locusts. And the locusts went up over all the land of Egypt, and rested in all the borders of Egypt; very grievous were they; before them there were no such locusts as they, neither after them shall be such. For they covered the face of the whole earth, so that the land was darkened; and they did eat every herb of the land, and all the fruit

The Exodus   Moses

of the trees which the hail had left: and there remained not any green thing, either tree or herb of the field, through all the land of Egypt. Then Pharaoh called for Moses and Aaron in haste; and he said, I have sinned against the LORD your God, and against you. Now therefore forgive, I pray thee, my sin only this once, and intreat the LORD your God, that he may take away from me this death only. And he went out from Pharaoh, and intreated the LORD. And the LORD turned an exceeding strong west wind, which took up the locusts, and drove them into the Red Sea; there remained not one locust in all the border of Egypt. But the LORD hardened Pharaoh's heart, and he did not let the children of Israel go.

And the LORD said unto Moses, Stretch out thine hand toward heaven, that there may be darkness over the land of Egypt, even darkness which may be felt. And Moses stretched forth his hand toward heaven; and there was a thick darkness in all the land of Egypt three days; they saw not one another, neither rose any from his place for three days: but all the children of Israel had light in their dwellings. And Pharaoh called unto Moses, and said, Go ye, serve the LORD; only let your flocks and your herds be stayed: let your little ones also go with you. And Moses said, Thou must also give into our hand sacrifices and burnt offerings, that we may sacrifice unto the LORD our God. Our cattle also shall go with us; there shall not an hoof be left behind; for thereof must we take to serve the LORD our God; and we know not with what we must serve the LORD, until we come thither. But the LORD hardened Pharaoh's heart, and he would not let them go. And Pharaoh said unto him, Get thee from me, take heed to thyself, see my face no more; for in the day thou seest my face thou shalt die. And Moses said, Thou hast spoken well; I will see thy face again no more.

And the LORD said unto Moses, yet one plague more will I bring upon Pharaoh, and upon Egypt; afterwards he will let you go hence: when he shall let you go, he shall surely thrust you out hence altogether. Speak now in the ears of the people, and let them ask every man of his neighbour, and every woman of her neighbour, jewels of silver, and jewels of gold. And the LORD gave the people favour in the sight of the Egyptians. Moreover the man Moses was very great in the land of Egypt, in the sight of Pharaoh's servants, and in the sight of the people.

And Moses said, Thus saith the LORD, About midnight will I go out into the midst of Egypt: and all the firstborn in the land of Egypt shall die, from the firstborn of Pharaoh that sitteth upon his throne, even unto the firstborn of the maidservant that is behind the mill; and all the firstborn of cattle. And there shall be a great cry throughout all the land of Egypt, such as there hath been none like it, nor shall be like it any more. But against any of the children of Israel shall not a dog move his tongue, against man or beast: that ye may know how that the

The Exodus ~ Moses

LORD doth put a difference between the Egyptians and Israel. And all these thy servants shall come down unto me, and bow down themselves unto me, saying, Get thee out, and all the people that follow thee: and after that I will go out. And he went out from Pharaoh in hot anger.

Then Moses called for all the elders of Israel, and said unto them, Draw out, and take you lambs according to your families, and kill the passover. And ye shall take a bunch of hyssop, and dip it in the blood that is in the bason, and strike the lintel and the two side posts with the blood that is in the bason; and none of you shall go out of the door of his house until the morning. For the LORD will pass through to smite the Egyptians; and when he seeth the blood upon the lintel, and on the two side posts, the LORD will pass over the door, and will not suffer the destroyer to come in unto your houses to smite you. And ye shall observe this thing for an ordinance to thee and to thy sons for ever.

And it came to pass at midnight, that the LORD smote all the firstborn in the land of Egypt, from the firstborn of Pharaoh that sat on his throne unto the firstborn of the captive that was in the dungeon; and all the firstborn of cattle. And Pharaoh rose up in the night, he, and all his servants, and all the Egyptians; and there was a great cry in Egypt; for there was not a house where there was not one dead. And he called for Moses and

Aaron by night, and said, Rise up, get you forth from among my people, both ye and the children of Israel; and go, serve the LORD, as ye have said. Take both your flocks and your herds, as ye have said, and be gone; and bless me also. And the Egyptians were urgent upon the people, to send them out of the land in haste; for they said, We be all dead men. And the people took their dough before it was leavened, their kneadingtroughs being bound up in their clothes upon their shoulders. And the children of Israel did according to the word of Moses; and they asked of the Egyptians jewels of silver, and jewels of gold, and raiment: and the LORD gave the people favour in the sight of the Egyptians, so that they let them have what they asked. And they spoiled the Egyptians.

Overthrow of the Egyptians at the Red Sea

And it was told the king of Egypt that the people were fled: and the heart of Pharaoh and of his servants was changed towards the people, and they said, What is this we have done, that we have let Israel go from serving us? And he made ready his chariot, and took his people with him: and he took six hundred chosen chariots, and all the chariots of Egypt, and captains over all of them. And the LORD hardened the heart of Pharaoh king of Egypt, and he pursued after the children of Israel: for the children of Israel went out with an high hand. And the

The Exodus   Moses

Egyptians pursued after them, all the horses and chariots of Pharaoh, and his horsemen, and his army, and overtook them encamping by the sea. And when Pharaoh drew nigh, the children of Israel lifted up their eyes, and, behold, the Egyptians marched after them; and they were sore afraid: and the children of Israel cried out unto the LORD. And they said unto Moses, Because there were no graves in Egypt, hast thou taken us away to die in the wilderness? wherefore hast thou dealt thus with us, to bring us forth out of Egypt? Is not this the word that we spake unto thee in Egypt, saying, Let us alone, that we may serve the Egyptians? For it were better for us to serve the Egyptians, than that we should die in the wilderness. And Moses said unto the people, Fear ye not, stand still, and see the salvation of the LORD, which he will work for you today: for the Egyptians whom ye have seen today, ye shall see them again no more for ever. The LORD shall fight for you, and ye shall hold your peace.

And the LORD said unto Moses, Wherefore criest thou unto me? speak unto the children of Israel, that they go forward. And lift thou up thy rod, and stretch out thine hand over the sea, and divide it: and the children of Israel shall go into the midst of the sea on dry ground. And I, behold, I will harden the hearts of the Egyptians, and they shall go in after them: and I will get me honour upon Pharaoh, and upon all his host, upon his chariots, and upon his horsemen. And the Egyptians shall know that I am the LORD, when I have gotten me honour upon Pharaoh, upon his chariots, and upon his horsemen. And the angel of God, which went before the camp of Israel, removed and went behind them; and the pillar of cloud removed from before them, and stood behind them: and it came between the camp of Egypt and the camp of Israel; and there was the cloud and the darkness, yet gave it light by night: and the one came not near the other all the night. And Moses stretched out his hand over the sea; and the LORD caused the sea to go back by a strong east wind all the night, and made the sea dry land, and the waters were divided. And the children of Israel went into the midst of the sea upon the dry ground: and the waters were a wall unto them on their right hand, and on their left. And the Egyptians pursued, and went in after them into the midst of the sea, all Pharaoh's horses, his chariots, and his horsemen. And it came to pass in the morning watch, that the LORD looked forth upon the host of the Egyptians through the pillar of fire and of cloud, and discomfited the host of the Egyptians. And he took off their chariot wheels, that they drave them heavily; so that the Egyptians said, Let us flee from the face of Israel; for the LORD fighteth for them against the Egyptians.

And the LORD said unto Moses, Stretch out thine hand over the sea, that the waters may come again upon the

Egyptians, upon their chariots and upon their horsemen. And Moses stretched forth his hand over the sea, and the sea returned to its strength when the morning appeared; and the Egyptians fled against it; and the LORD overthrew the Egyptians in the midst of the sea. And the waters returned, and covered the chariots, and the horsemen, even all the host of Pharaoh that went in after them into the sea; there remained not so much as one of them.

Thus the LORD saved Israel that day out of the hand of the Egyptians; and Israel saw the Egyptians dead upon the sea shore. And the people believed in the LORD and in his servant Moses.

Then sang Moses and the children of Israel this song unto the LORD.

Song of Moses and Miriam

ALL TOGETHER

I will sing unto the LORD, for he hath triumphed gloriously:
The horse and his rider hath he thrown into the sea.
The LORD is my strength and song,
    And he is become my salvation:
This is my God, and I will praise him;
    My father's God, and I will exalt him.

1

MEN

The LORD is a man of war:
  The LORD is his name.
Pharaoh's chariots and his host hath he cast into the sea:
  And his chosen captains are sunk in the Red Sea.
The deeps cover them:
  They went down into the depths like a stone.

WOMEN

Sing ye to the LORD, for he hath triumphed gloriously:
  The horse and his rider hath he thrown into the sea.

2

MEN

Thy right hand, O LORD, is glorious in power,
  Thy right hand, O LORD, dasheth in pieces the enemy.
And in the greatness of thine excellency thou overthrowest
    them that rise up against thee:
  Thou sendest forth thy wrath, it consumeth them as
    stubble.
And with the blast of thy nostrils the waters were piled up,
  The floods stood upright as an heap;
  The deeps were congealed in the heart of the sea.

The Exodus   Moses

The enemy said, I will pursue, I will overtake, I will divide
    the spoil:
    My lust shall be satisfied upon them;
    I will draw my sword, my hand shall destroy them.
Thou didst blow with thy wind, the sea covered them:
    They sank as lead in the mighty waters.

WOMEN

Sing ye to the LORD, for he hath triumphed gloriously:
    The horse and his rider hath he thrown into the sea.

3

MEN

Who is like unto thee, O LORD, among the gods?
    Who is like thee, glorious in holiness,
    Fearful in praises, doing wonders?
Thou stretchedst out thy right hand,
    The earth swallowed them.
Thou in thy mercy hast led the people which thou hast
    redeemed:
    Thou hast guided them in thy strength to thy holy
        habitation.
The peoples have heard, they tremble:
    Pangs have taken hold on the inhabitants of Philistia.

Then were the dukes of Edom amazed;
> The mighty men of Moab, trembling taketh hold upon them:

All the inhabitants of Canaan are melted away.
> Terror and dread falleth upon them;

By the greatness of thine arm they are as still as a stone;
> Till thy people pass over, O Lord,
> Till the people pass over which thou hast purchased.

Thou shalt bring them in, and plant them in the mountain of thine inheritance,
The place, O Lord, which thou hast made for thee to dwell in,
> The sanctuary, O Lord, which thy hands have established.

The Lord shall reign for ever and ever.

WOMEN

Sing ye to the Lord, for he hath triumphed gloriously:
> *The horse and his rider hath he thrown into the sea.*

ii

Law of the Ten Commandments from Sinai

And the LORD said unto Moses, Go unto the people, and sanctify them today and tomorrow, and let them wash their garments, and be ready against the third day: for the third day the LORD will come down in the sight of all the people upon mount Sinai. And thou shalt set bounds unto the people round about, saying, Take heed to yourselves, that ye go not up into the mount, or touch the border of it: whosoever toucheth the mount shall be surely put to death: no hand shall touch him, but he shall surely be stoned, or shot through; whether it be beast or man, it shall not live: when the trumpet soundeth long, they shall come up to the mount. And Moses went down from the mount unto the people, and sanctified the people; and they washed their garments. And he said unto the people, Be ready against the third day.

And it came to pass on the third day, when it was morning, that there were thunders and lightnings, and a thick cloud upon the mount, and the voice of a trumpet exceeding loud; and all the people that were in the camp trembled. And Moses brought forth the people out of the camp to meet God; and they stood at the nether part of the mount. And mount Sinai was altogether on smoke, because the Lord descended upon it in fire: and the smoke thereof ascended as the smoke of a furnace, and the whole mount quaked greatly. And when the voice of the trumpet waxed louder and louder, Moses spake, and God answered him by a voice.

And God spake all these words, saying:

I am the Lord thy God, which brought thee out of the land of Egypt, out of the house of bondage.

THOU SHALT HAVE NONE OTHER GODS BEFORE ME.

THOU SHALT NOT MAKE UNTO THEE A GRAVEN IMAGE, nor the likeness of any form that is in heaven above, or that is in the earth beneath, or that is in the water under the earth: thou shalt not bow down thyself unto them, nor serve them: for I the Lord thy God am a jealous God, visiting the iniquity of the fathers upon the children, upon the third and upon the fourth generation of them that hate me; and shewing mercy unto thousands, of them that love me and keep my commandments.

THOU SHALT NOT TAKE THE NAME OF THE LORD THY GOD IN VAIN; for the Lord will not hold him guiltless that taketh his name in vain.

REMEMBER THE SABBATH DAY, TO KEEP IT HOLY. Six days shalt thou labour, and do all thy work: but the seventh day is a sabbath unto the Lord thy God: in it thou shalt not do any work, thou, nor thy son, nor thy daughter, thy manservant, nor thy maidservant, nor thy cattle, nor thy stranger that is within thy gates: for in six days the LORD made heaven and earth, the sea, and all that in them is, and rested the seventh day: wherefore the LORD blessed the sabbath day, and hallowed it.

HONOUR THY FATHER AND THY MOTHER: that thy days may be long upon the land which the LORD thy God giveth thee.

THOU SHALT DO NO MURDER.

THOU SHALT NOT COMMIT ADULTERY.

THOU SHALT NOT STEAL.

THOU SHALT NOT BEAR FALSE WITNESS against thy neighbour.

THOU SHALT NOT COVET thy neighbour's house, thou shalt not covet thy neighbour's wife, nor his manservant, nor his maidservant, nor his ox, nor his ass, nor any thing that is thy neighbour's.

And all the people saw the thunderings, and the lightnings, and the voice of the trumpet, and the mountain smoking: and when the people saw it, they trembled, and stood afar off. And they said unto Moses, Speak thou with us, and we will hear: but let not God speak with us, lest we die. And Moses said unto the people, Fear not: for God is come to prove you, and that his fear may be before you, that ye sin not. And the people stood afar off, and Moses drew near unto the thick darkness where God was.

iii

The Witness of Balaam to Israel

And Moab was sore afraid of the people of Israel, because they were many; and Moab said, Now shall this multitude lick up all that is round about us, as the ox licketh up the grass of the field. And Balak the son of Zippor was king of Moab at that time. And he sent messengers unto Balaam, the son of Beor, to the land of the children of his people, to call him, saying, Behold, there is a people come out from Egypt; behold, they cover the face of the earth, and they abide over against me: come now therefore, I pray thee, curse me this people; for they are too mighty for me: peradventure I shall prevail, that we may smite them, and that I may drive them out of the land: for I know that he whom thou blessest is blessed, and he whom thou cursest is cursed. And the elders of Moab departed with the rewards of divination in their hand; and they came unto Balaam, and spake unto him the words of Balak. And he said unto them, Lodge here this night, and I will bring you word again, as the LORD shall speak unto me. And the princes of Moab abode with Balaam. And God came unto Balaam, and said, What men are these with thee? And

Balaam said unto God, Balak the son of Zippor, king of Moab, hath sent unto me, saying, Behold, the people that is come out of Egypt, it covereth the face of the earth: now, come curse me them; peradventure I shall be able to fight against them, and shall drive them out. And God said unto Balaam, Thou shalt not go with them; thou shalt not curse the people: for they are blessed. And Balaam rose up in the morning, and said unto the princes of Balak, Get you into your land: for the LORD refuseth to give me leave to go with you.

And the princes of Moab rose up, and they went unto Balak, and said, Balaam refuseth to come with us. And Balak sent yet again princes, more, and more honourable than they. And they came to Balaam, and said to him, Thus saith Balak, the son of Zippor, Let nothing, I pray thee, hinder thee from coming unto me: for I will promote thee unto very great honour, and whatsoever thou sayest unto me I will do: come therefore, I pray thee, curse me this people. And Balaam answered and said unto the servants of Balak, If Balak would give me his house full of silver and gold, I cannot go beyond the word of the LORD my God, to do less or more. Now therefore, I pray you, tarry ye also here this night, that I may know what the LORD will speak unto me more. And God came unto Balaam at night, and said unto him, If the men be come to call thee, rise up, go with them; but only the word which I speak unto thee, that shalt thou do.

Balaam

So Balaam went with the princes of Balak. And when Balak heard that Balaam was come, he went out to meet him unto the city of Moab, which is in the utmost part of the border. And Balak said unto Balaam, Did I not earnestly send unto thee to call thee? wherefore camest thou not unto me? am I not able indeed to promote thee to honour? And Balaam said unto Balak, Lo, I am come unto thee: have I now any power at all to speak anything? the word that God putteth in my mouth, that shall I speak.

And it came to pass in the morning, that Balak took Balaam, and brought him up into the high places of Baal, and he saw from thence the utmost part of the people. And Balaam said unto Balak, Build me here seven altars, and prepare me here seven bullocks and seven rams. And Balak did as Balaam had spoken; and Balak and Balaam offered on every altar a bullock and a ram. And Balaam said unto Balak, Stand by thy burnt offering, and I will go; peradventure the LORD will come to meet me: and whatsoever he sheweth me I will tell thee. And he went to a bare height. And God met Balaam: and he said unto him, I have prepared the seven altars, and I have offered up a bullock and a ram on every altar. And the LORD put a word in Balaam's mouth, and said, Return unto Balak, and thus thou shalt speak. And he returned unto him, and, lo, he stood by his burnt offering, he, and all the princes of Moab. And he took up his parable, and said:

The Exodus   Balaam

From Aram hath Balak brought me,
    The king of Moab from the mountains of the East:
Come, curse me Jacob,
    And come, defy Israel.
How shall I curse, whom God hath not cursed?
    And how shall I defy, whom the LORD hath not defied?
For from the top of the rocks I see him,
    And from the hills I behold him:
Lo, it is a people that dwell alone,
    And shall not be reckoned among the nations.
Who can count the dust of Jacob,
    Or number the fourth part of Israel?
Let me die the death of the righteous,
    And let my last end be like his!

And Balak said unto Balaam, What hast thou done unto me? I took thee to curse mine enemies, and, behold, thou hast blessed them altogether. And he answered and said, Must I not take heed to speak that which the LORD putteth in my mouth?

And Balak said unto him, Come, I pray thee, with me unto another place, from whence thou mayest see them; thou shalt see but the utmost part of them, and shalt not see them all: and curse me them from thence. And he took him into the field of Zophim, to the top of Pisgah, and built seven altars, and offered up a bullock and a ram on every altar. And he said unto Balak, Stand here by thy burnt offering, while I meet the LORD yonder. And the LORD met Balaam, and put a word in his mouth, and said, Return unto Balak, and thus shalt thou speak. And he came to him, and, lo, he stood by his burnt offering, and the princes of Moab with him. And Balak said unto him, What hath the LORD spoken? And he took up his parable, and said:

> Rise up, Balak, and hear;
>   Hearken unto me, thou son of Zippor:
> God is not a man, that he should lie;
>   Neither the son of man, that he should repent:
> Hath he said, and shall he not do it?
>   Or hath he spoken, and shall he not make it good?
> Behold, I have received commandment to bless:
>   And he hath blessed, and I cannot reverse it.
> He hath not beheld iniquity in Jacob,
>   Neither hath he seen perverseness in Israel:
> The LORD his God is with him,
>   And the shout of a king is among them.
> God bringeth them forth out of Egypt;
>   He hath as it were the strength of the wild-ox.
> Surely there is no enchantment against Jacob,
>   Neither is there any divination against Israel:
>   Now shall it be said of Jacob and of Israel, What hath God wrought!

> Behold, the people riseth up as a lioness,
>   And as a lion doth he lift himself up:
> He shall not lie down until he eat of the prey,
>   And drink the blood of the slain.

And Balak said unto Balaam, Neither curse them at all, nor bless them at all. But Balaam answered and said unto Balak, Told not I thee, saying, All that the LORD speaketh, that I must do?

And Balak said unto Balaam, Come now, I will take thee unto another place; peradventure, it will please God that thou mayest curse me them from thence. And Balak took Balaam unto the top of Peor, that looketh down upon the desert. And Balaam said unto Balak, Build me here seven altars, and prepare me here seven bullocks and seven rams. And Balak did as Balaam had said, and offered up a bullock and a ram on every altar. And when Balaam saw that it pleased the LORD to bless Israel, he went not, as at the other times, to meet with enchantments, but he set his face toward the wilderness. And Balaam lifted up his eyes, and he saw Israel dwelling according to their tribes; and the spirit of God came upon him. And he took up his parable, and said:

> Balaam the son of Beor saith,
>   And the man whose eye is opened saith:
> He saith, which heareth the words of God,

> Which seeth the vision of the Almighty,
>> Falling down, and having his eyes open:
>
> How goodly are thy tents, O Jacob,
>> Thy tabernacles, O Israel!
> As valleys are they spread forth,
>> As gardens by the river side,
> As lign-aloes which the LORD hath planted,
>> As cedar trees beside the waters.
> Water shall flow from his buckets,
>> And his seed shall be in many waters,
> And his king shall be higher than Agag,
>> And his kingdom shall be exalted.
> God bringeth him forth out of Egypt;
>> He hath as it were the strength of the wild-ox:
> He shall eat up the nations his adversaries,
>> And shall break their bones in pieces,
>> And smite them through with his arrows.
> He couched, he lay down as a lion,
>> And as a lioness; who shall rouse him up?
> Blessed be every one that blesseth thee,
>> And cursed be every one that curseth thee.

And Balak's anger was kindled against Balaam, and he smote his hands together: and Balak said unto Balaam, I called thee to curse mine enemies, and, behold, thou hast altogether blessed them these three times. Therefore now flee thou to thy place: I thought to promote thee unto great honour; but, lo, the LORD hath kept thee back from honour. And Balaam said unto Balak, Spake I not also to thy messengers which thou sentest unto me, saying, If Balak would give me his house full of silver and gold, I cannot go beyond the word of the LORD, to do either good or bad of mine own mind; what the LORD speaketh, that will I speak? And now, behold, I go unto my people: come, and I will advertise thee what this people shall do to thy people in the latter days. And he took up his parable, and said:

> Balaam the son of Beor saith,
>   And the man whose eye is opened saith:
> He saith, which heareth the words of God,
>   And knoweth the knowledge of the Most High,
> Which seeth the vision of the Almighty,
>   Falling down, and having his eyes open:

> I see him, but not now:
>   I behold him, but not nigh:
> There shall come forth a star out of Jacob,
>   And a sceptre shall rise out of Israel,
> And shall smite through the corners of Moab,
>   And break down all the sons of tumult.
> And Edom shall be a possession,

Seir also shall be a possession, which were his enemies;
While Israel doeth valiantly.

And Balaam rose up, and went and returned to his place:
and Balak also went his way.

The Exodus ❧   Notes

Notes to The Exodus

i. Note the preparation of Moses for his future career by his education at court in the learning of the age. — **Page 79.** *Abomination of the Egyptians:* that is, cattle: which the Egyptian religion regarded as objects of worship, Moses as wicked idols. — **Page 80.** *Blains:* an old word for blister. — **Page 81.** *The LORD hardened the heart of Pharaoh.* In the earlier stages of this story it is said that *Pharaoh's heart was hardened*, or that *Pharaoh hardened his heart;* in the later parts the expression is used that God *hardened Pharaoh's heart.* Voluntary yielding to evil produces in time a tendency to evil that can hardly be resisted. What happens by a law of God's providence may properly be said to be done by God. — **Page 84.** *So be the LORD with you, as I will let you go,* etc.: Pharaoh is of course speaking ironically: May your God bless you as surely as I mean to grant your request: that is, not at all. — **Page 86.** *See my face no more . . . I will see thy face again no more:* the context shows that the phrase *see Pharaoh's face* is used in the sense of coming before Pharaoh with a petition. When Moses comes the next time, he makes no petition, but only utters a threat. — **Page 91.** This Song was probably performed thus: the Men, headed by Aaron, alternated with the Women headed by Aaron's sister Miriam. The women's part is a refrain coming over again and again, and was accompanied with timbrel music and dancing. — **Page 93.** *Philistia . . . Edom . . . Moab:* Edom and Moab were peoples the Israelites were to encounter in the wilderness, Philistia was the chief of their future foes in Canaan. Poetically these people are imagined as trembling before this deliverance of Israel at the Red Sea, which was the first step towards their future triumphs.

ii. *Moses spake, and God answered him by a voice.* The probable meaning of these words is that only the commandments themselves [here printed in capitals] were heard from the voice of God: the rest was added by Moses as explanation.

iii. For the understanding of this famous story certain points must be carefully noted. — 1. Balaam is a worshipper of the God of Israel, probably in the region from which Abraham originally came. In this worship he is perfectly sincere; and he has the gift of prophecy. But prophecy comes only at special times of intercourse with God: outside such times Balaam is a worldly man, adapting himself to those about him. Outsiders like Balak cannot understand so spiritual a thing as prophecy, but suppose Balaam's power to be magic or enchantment: *whom* [ ] *. . . cursest he is cursed:* and he sends messengers *with the rewards of divination* (or magic) in their hand. [From other parts of the Bible history we learn that worldliness finally triumphed in Balaam, he fell into grave sin and perished.] — 2. Page 100. *And he took up his parable, and said.* The word *parable* is applied in Scripture to speech that differs in any way from ordinary speech, as when a story is substituted for discourse, or verse for prose. The verse of Scripture is made, not by rhyme or number of syllables in a line, but by each line having another line (or even two) that runs parallel with it. Prose would be: *For from the top of the rocks*

The Exodus   Notes

I see him: lo, it is a people that dwell alone. To make this verse, each clause is supported by another similar clause:

> *For from the top of the rocks I see him,*
> *And from the hills I behold him;*
> *Lo, it is a people that dwell alone,*
> *And shall not be reckoned among the nations.*

[For fuller information on this subject see *Biblical Masterpieces*, p. 242.] — 3. **Page 103.** *He went not, as at other times, to meet with enchantments, but he set his face toward the wilderness.* Balak wants Balaam to curse Israel, believing his curse will be an enchantment that will wither them. Balaam for the sake of pleasing the king desires to do so, but only if God will allow him. Twice, after offering sacrifice, Balaam goes apart to hold secret intercourse with God: twice he feels Divine inspiration stirring him to bless the people he sees in the distance. When Balak makes a third attempt, and takes the prophet to a third point of view, Balaam is hopeless of getting permission to curse; he does not even go apart to be alone with God, but, where he is standing with Balak and the nobles of Moab, turns his face towards the part of the desert where the encampment of Israel is visible. It so happens that from this point of view the *regular order* of Israel's encampment becomes visible [a great contrast to the rude hordes of desert Bedouins]: this idea of order is the theme of his next outpouring, and is compared to valleys, riverside gardens, avenues of aloes. — 4. **Page 104.** *Water shall flow from his buckets:* another comparison for Israel's future greatness: that of a fountain from which different streams run in different directions.

BIBLE STORIES

THE JUDGES

INTRODUCTION TO THE JUDGES

In the third period of the Bible history the emigration of the Israelites had come to an end; they entered the Promised Land, and warred with the wicked nations who possessed it. They did not however drive them out; but, when they had conquered enough land, settled down with foes all around them.

Viewed in the light of Israel's mission as the Chosen People of God this period is a transitional stage in their history. Originally, Israel was unlike other nations in that it had no visible king. God was the ruler of Israel: and his will was made known to the people, at first by the fathers, and then by Moses, who is termed a 'prophet' — the word means 'interpreter of God.' But contact with the nations of Canaan produced in the Israelites a desire for visible kings to lead them in battle. They thus became a divided people: one part longing for these external kings, others standing for the rule of the invisible God. The first of these parties grew the stronger, and in its next period we shall find that Israel has a succession of kings.

In this middle period the government of Israel is described by the words, "Every man did that which was

Introduction   ⇥ Bible Stories

right in his own eyes." This does not however prove that there was no rule of any kind. "Every man" must be understood as every head of a family, or chief of a village; and the meaning is that there was only local or family authority, without any form of national government. But from time to time the oppression of surrounding foes forced common action upon the tribes of Israel. At such times there arose the 'Judges,' who have given their name to the period. This word as used in the Bible has not its modern meaning: it describes those who work out some act of justice or deliverance, often by war or violence. The Judges are thus the 'heroes' of Israel's history. As heroes and deliverers these Judges were obeyed by the whole nation, or large portions of it, for a time; and this temporary or partial rule of the Judges was thus a preparatory stage for the coming period when the whole nation was governed by a succession of regular kings.

The first leader of Israel at this time was Joshua: he however is not called a judge, but was the assistant and successor of the prophet Moses. Under Joshua the people entered the Promised Land and made their first conquests. His achievements are here represented by the story of the Crossing of the Jordan and the Capture of the first city, Jericho.

After a time we find Israel oppressed by a Canaanite king whose chariots of iron made him irresistible by a nation of foot soldiers. At this crisis a woman rose up to be judge; Deborah not only roused the people to resistance, but, choosing Barak as her commander-in-chief, herself marched against Sisera, and marvellously overthrew him. This incident has called forth a great poem (which is here given)—the Song of Deborah.

Another of our stories commemorates Gideon and his wonderful achievements against the Midianites, a horde of wandering peoples whose countless numbers made them almost irresistible. In the general history this represents an important point; for the people invited the victorious Gideon to be their king: but he was true to the principle that only the LORD should reign over Israel.

Jephthah, another judge, is commemorated by the strange story of Jephthah's Vow.

The chief foes of Israel were the Philistines, and in the constant wars with these some great champions arose. One of these was Samson, whose name is familiar to all time as a hero of vast strength and reckless valour. Samson's feats and his strange death form a succession of stories which are here given.

Of the judge Eli we only read in his old age. But under him there arose Samuel, the greatest prophet since Moses, and founder of a succession of prophets in the period that followed. The favourite stories of Samuel's birth and boyhood are here given. It is in his time that the desire of the people for a visible king reached its height, and Samuel received the Divine command to give *way to it. Accordingly, we have the story of the Anointing of Saul. But though Saul himself reigned, his unworthiness caused his family to be rejected from the succession to the throne; and Samuel anointed David, the first king from whom Israel was to trace its royal line. Saul resented this anointing of his successor in his lifetime; and the final story of this period relates the adventures of David under the persecution of Saul, and especially the friendship of David with Saul's son, Jonathan. The Battle of Gilboa brought about the death of Saul and Jonathan, and the accession of David to the throne of Israel.*

STORIES FROM THE JUDGES

    i. The Passage of the Jordan and Siege of Jericho
   ii. How the wily Gibeonites deceived Joshua
  iii. War of Deborah and Barak against Sisera
  iv. Feats of Gideon in the Midianite War
   v. Jephthah's Vow
  vi. Stories of Samson
      Samson's Wedding Feast
      The Jawbone of an Ass
      Samson and Delilah
      Death of Samson
  vii. The Old Man Eli and the Child Samuel
      Birth of Samuel
      The Child Samuel called to be a Prophet
      Loss of the Ark and Death of Eli
      Return of the Ark
 viii. The Anointing of Saul
  ix. The Rejection of Saul and Anointing of David
   x. The Feud of Saul and David and the Friendship of David and Jonathan
      David and Goliath
      How the Feud and the Friendship began
      The Escape by Night
      The Secret Meeting of David and Jonathan
      The Adventure of the Spear and Water-cruse
      The Battle of Gilboa

i

The Passage of the Jordan and Siege of Jericho

And Joshua rose up early in the morning, and came to Jordan, he and all the children of Israel; and they lodged there before they passed over.

And Joshua said unto the children of Israel, Come hither, and hear the words of the Lord your God. And Joshua said, Hereby ye shall know that the living God is among you. Behold, the ark of the covenant of the Lord of all the earth passeth over before you into Jordan. And it shall come to pass, when the soles of the feet of the priests that bear the ark of the Lord, the Lord of all the earth, shall rest in the waters of Jordan, that the waters of Jordan shall be cut off, even the waters that come down from above; and they shall stand in one heap. And it came to pass, when the people removed from their tents, to pass over Jordan, the priests that bare the ark of the covenant being before the people; and when they that bare the ark were come unto Jordan, and the feet of the priests that bare the ark were dipped in the brink of the water, (for Jordan overfloweth all its banks all the time of harvest,) that the waters which came down from above stood, and rose up in one heap, a great way off: and those that went down toward the sea were wholly cut off: and the people passed over right against Jericho. And the priests that bare the ark of the covenant of the LORD stood firm on dry ground in the midst of Jordan, and all Israel passed over on dry ground, until all the nation were passed clean over Jordan. And it came to pass, when the priests that bare the ark of the covenant of the LORD were come up out of the midst of Jordan, and the soles of the priests' feet were lifted up unto the dry ground, that the waters of Jordan returned unto their place, and went over all its banks, as aforetime. And the people came up out of Jordan on the tenth day of the first month, and encamped in Gilgal, on the east border of Jericho.

And it came to pass, when Joshua was by Jericho, that he lifted up his eyes and looked, and, behold, there stood a man over against him with his sword drawn in his hand: and Joshua went unto him, and said unto him, Art thou for us, or for our adversaries? And he said, Nay; but as captain of the host of the LORD am I now come. And Joshua fell on his face to the earth, and did worship, and said unto him, What saith my Lord unto his servant? and the captain of the LORD's host said unto Joshua, Put off thy shoe from off thy foot; for the place whereon thou standest is holy. And Joshua did so. (Now Jericho was straitly shut up because of the children of Israel: none

The Judges ❧   Joshua

went out, and none came in.) And the LORD said unto Joshua, See, I have given into thine hand Jericho, and the king thereof, and the mighty men of valour. And ye shall compass the city, all the men of war, going about the city once. Thus shalt thou do six days. And seven priests shall bear seven trumpets of rams' horns before the ark: and the seventh day ye shall compass the city seven times, and the priests shall blow with the trumpets. And it shall be, that when they make a long blast with the ram's horn, and when ye hear the sound of the trumpet, all the people shall shout with a great shout; and the wall of the city shall fall down flat, and the people shall go up every man straight before him.

And Joshua rose early in the morning, and the priests took up the ark of the LORD. And the seven priests bearing the seven trumpets of rams' horns before the ark of the LORD went on continually, and blew with the trumpets: and the armed men went before them; and the rearward came after the ark of the LORD, the priests blowing with the trumpets as they went. And the second day they compassed the city once, and returned into the camp: so they did six days. And it came to pass on the seventh day, that they rose early at the dawning of the day, and compassed the city after the same manner seven times: only on that day they compassed the city seven times. And it came to pass at the seventh time, when the priests blew with the trumpets, Joshua said unto the people, Shout: for the LORD hath given you the city. So the people shouted, and the priests blew with the trumpets: and it came to pass, when the people heard the sound of the trumpet, that the people shouted with a great shout, and the wall fell down flat, so that the people went up into the city, every man straight before him, and they took the city.

ii

How the wily Gibeonites deceived Joshua

And it came to pass, when the inhabitants of Gibeon heard what Joshua had done unto Jericho and to Ai, they did work wilily, and went and made as if they had been ambassadors, and took old sacks upon their asses, and wine-skins, old and rent and bound up; and old shoes and clouted upon their feet, and old garments upon them; and all the bread of their provision was dry and was become mouldy. And they went to Joshua unto the camp at Gilgal, and said unto him, and to the men of Israel, We are come from a far country: now therefore make ye a covenant with us. And the men of Israel said unto the Hivites, Peradventure ye dwell among us; and how shall we make a covenant with you? And they said unto Joshua, We are thy servants. And Joshua said unto

The Judges ~ Joshua

them, Who are ye? and from whence come ye? And they said unto him, From a very far country thy servants are come because of the name of the LORD thy God: for we have heard the fame of him, and all that he did in Egypt, and all that he did to the two kings of the Amorites, that were beyond Jordan, to Sihon king of Heshbon, and to Og king of Bashan. And our elders and all the inhabitants of our country spake to us, saying, Take provision in your hand for the journey, and go to meet them, and say unto them, We are your servants: and now make ye a covenant with us. This our bread we took hot for our provision out of our houses on the day we came forth to go unto you; but now, behold, it is dry, and is become mouldy: and these wine-skins, which we filled, were new; and, behold, they be rent: and these our garments and our shoes are become old by reason of the very long journey. And the men took of their provision, and asked not counsel at the mouth of the LORD. And Joshua made peace with them, and made a covenant with them, to let them live: and the princes of the congregation sware unto them.

And it came to pass at the end of three days after they had made a covenant with them, that they heard that they were their neighbours, and that they dwelt among them. And the children of Israel journeyed, and came unto their cities on the third day. And the children of Israel smote them not, because the princes of the congregation had sworn unto them by the LORD, the God of

Israel. And all the congregation murmured against the princes. But all the princes said unto all the congregation, We have sworn unto them by the LORD, the God of Israel: now therefore we may not touch them. This we will do to them, and let them live; lest wrath be upon us, because of the oath which we sware unto them. And the princes said unto them, Let them live: so they became hewers of wood and drawers of water unto all the congregation; as the princes had spoken unto them. And Joshua called for them, and he spake unto them, saying, Wherefore have ye beguiled us, saying, We are very far from you; when ye dwell among us? Now therefore ye are cursed, and there shall never fail to be of you bondmen, both hewers of wood and drawers of water for the house of my God. And they answered Joshua, and said, Because it was certainly told thy servants, how that the LORD thy God commanded his servant Moses to give you all the land, and to destroy all the inhabitants of the land from before you; therefore we were sore afraid for our lives because of you, and have done this thing. And now, behold, we are in thine hand: as it seemeth good and right unto thee to do unto us, do. And so did he unto them, and delivered them out of the hand of the children of Israel, that they slew them not. And Joshua made them that day hewers of wood and drawers of water for the congregation, and for the altar of the LORD, unto this day, in the place which he should choose.

iii

War of Deborah and Barak against Sisera

And the children of Israel again did that which was evil in the sight of the LORD. And the LORD sold them into the hand of Jabin king of Canaan, that reigned in Hazor; the captain of whose host was Sisera. And the children of Israel cried unto the LORD: for he had nine hundred chariots of iron: and twenty years he mightily oppressed the children of Israel.

Now Deborah, a prophetess, the wife of Lappidoth, she judged Israel at that time. And she dwelt under the palm tree of Deborah in the hill country of Ephraim: and the children of Israel came up to her for judgement. And she sent and called Barak the son of Abinoam out of Kedesh-naphtali, and said unto him, Hath not the LORD, the God of Israel, commanded, saying, Go and draw unto mount Tabor, and take with thee ten thousand men of the children of Naphtali and of the children of Zebulun? And I will draw unto thee to the river Kishon Sisera, the captain of Jabin's army, with his chariots and his multitude; and I will deliver him into thine hand. And Barak said unto her, If thou wilt go with me, then I will go: but if thou wilt not go with me, I will not go. And she said, I will surely go with thee: notwithstanding the journey that thou takest shall not be for thine honour; for the LORD shall sell Sisera into the hand of a woman. And Deborah arose, and went with Barak to Kedesh. And Barak called Zebulun and Naphtali together to Kedesh; and there went up ten thousand men at his feet: and Deborah went up with him.

Now Heber the Kenite had severed himself from the Kenites, even from the children of Hobab the brother in law of Moses, and had pitched his tent as far as the oak in Zaanannim, which is by Kedesh. And they told Sisera that Barak the son of Abinoam was gone up to mount Tabor. And Sisera gathered together all his chariots, even nine hundred chariots of iron, and all the people that were with him, unto the river Kishon. And Deborah said unto Barak, Up; for this is the day in which the LORD hath delivered Sisera into thine hand: is not the LORD gone out before thee? So Barak went down from mount Tabor, and ten thousand men after him. And the LORD discomfited Sisera, and all his chariots, and all his host, with the edge of the sword before Barak; and Sisera lighted down from his chariot, and fled away on his feet. But Barak pursued after the chariots, and after the host: and all the host of Sisera fell by the edge of the sword; there was not a man left.

Howbeit Sisera fled away on his feet to the tent of Jael the wife of Heber the Kenite: for there was peace between Jabin the king of Hazor and the house of Heber the Kenite. And Jael went out to meet Sisera, and said unto him, Turn in, my lord, turn in to me; fear not. And he turned in unto her into the tent, and she covered him with a rug. And he said unto her, Give me, I pray thee, a little water to drink; for I am thirsty. And she opened a bottle of milk, and gave him drink, and covered him. And he said unto her, Stand in the door of the tent, and it shall be, when any man doth come and inquire of thee, and say, Is there any man here? that thou shalt say, No. Then Jael, Heber's wife, took a tent-pin, and took an hammer in her hand, and went softly unto him, and smote the pin into his temples, and it pierced through into the ground; for he was in a deep sleep; so he swooned and died. And, behold, as Barak pursued Sisera, Jael came out to meet him, and said unto him, Come, and I will shew thee the man whom thou seekest. And he came unto her; and, behold, Sisera lay dead, and the tent-pin was in his temples.

So God subdued on that day Jabin the king of Canaan before the children of Israel. Then sang Deborah and Barak on that day, saying:

Song of Deborah

Men. *For that the leaders took the lead in Israel —*
Women. *For that the people offered themselves willingly —*
All. *Bless ye the* LORD.

Prelude

Men.   Hear, O ye kings —
Women. Give ear, O ye princes —
Men.   I, even I, will sing unto the LORD —
Women. I will sing praise to the LORD, the God of Israel.

All.   LORD, when thou wentest forth out of Seir,
        When thou marchedst out of the field of Edom,
      The earth trembled, the heavens also dropped,
        Yea, the clouds dropped water.
      The mountains flowed down at the presence of the LORD,
        Even yon Sinai at the presence of the LORD, the God of Israel.

1. The Desolation

Men.   In the days of Shamgar the son of Anath,
        In the days of Jael,
      The highways were unoccupied,
        And the travellers walked through byways;
      The rulers ceased in Israel,
        They ceased —

The Judges — Deborah

Women.	Until that I, Deborah, arose,
	That I arose a mother in Israel.
	They chose new gods;
	Then was war in the gates:
	Was there a shield or spear seen
	Among forty thousand in Israel?
Men.	*My heart is toward the governors of Israel —*
Women.	*Ye that offered yourselves willingly among the people —*
All.	*Bless ye the* LORD*!*
Men.	*Tell of it, ye that ride on white asses,*
	Ye that sit on rich carpets,
	And ye that walk by the way: —
Women.	*Far from the noise of archers,*
	In the places of drawing water: —
All.	*There shall they rehearse the righteous acts of the* LORD*,*
	Even the righteous acts of his rule in Israel.

2. THE MUSTER

All.	Then the people of the LORD went down to the gates —
(*Men.*	*Awake, awake, Deborah,*
	Awake, awake, utter a song: —
Women.	*Arise, Barak,*
	And lead thy captivity captive, thou son of Abinoam.)

All.	Then came down a remnant of the nobles,
	The people of the L<small>ORD</small> came down for me against the mighty.
Women.	Out of Ephraim came down they whose root is in Amalek —
Men.	After thee, Benjamin, among thy peoples —
Women.	Out of Machir came down governors —
Men.	And out of Zebulun they that handle the marshal's staff —
Women.	And the princes of Issachar were with Deborah —
Men.	As was Issachar, so was Barak:
All.	Into the valley they rushed forth at his feet.
Men.	By the watercourses of Reuben There were great resolves of heart.
Women.	Why satest thou among the sheepfolds, To hear the pipings for the flocks?
Men.	At the watercourses of Reuben There were great searchings of heart!
Women.	Gilead abode beyond Jordan —
Men.	And Dan, why did he remain in ships? —
Women.	Asher sat still at the haven of the sea, And abode by his creeks.
Men.	Zebulun was a people that jeoparded their lives unto the death, And Naphtali upon the high places of the field.

The Judges   Deborah

3. THE BATTLE AND ROUT

Men.   The kings came and fought;
           Then fought the kings of Canaan,
      In Taanach by the waters of Megiddo: —
           They took no gain of money!

Women.   They fought from heaven,
           The stars in their courses fought against
              Sisera.
      The river Kishon swept them away, —
           That ancient river, the river Kishon!

Men.   O my soul, march on with strength!
           Then did the horsehoofs stamp
      By reason of the pransings,
           The pransings of their strong ones.

Women.   Curse ye Meroz, said the angel of the LORD,
           Curse ye bitterly the inhabitants thereof;
      Because they came not to the help of the LORD,
           To the help of the LORD against the
              mighty!

4. THE RETRIBUTION

Men.   Blessed above women shall Jael be, the wife of
           Heber the Kenite,
      Blessed shall she be above women in the
           tent!

He asked water, and she gave him milk;
 She brought him butter in a lordly dish.
She put her hand to the nail,
 And her right hand to the workman's hammer;
And with the hammer she smote Sisera.
She smote through his head,
 Yea, she pierced and struck though his temples.
At her feet he bowed, he fell, he lay:
At her feet he bowed, he fell:
 Where he bowed, there he fell down dead!

Women. Through the window she looked forth, and cried,
 The mother of Sisera, through the lattice,
" Why is his chariot so long in coming?
 Why tarry the wheels of his chariots?"
Her wise ladies answered her,
 Yea, she returned answer to herself,
" Have they not found,
Have they not divided the spoil?
 A damsel, two damsels to every man;
To Sisera a spoil of divers colours,
A spoil of divers colours of embroidery,
 Of divers colours of embroidery on both sides, on the necks of the spoil!"

All.   So let thine enemies perish, O LORD:
>   But let them that love him be as the sun
>   when he goeth forth in his might!

iv

Feats of Gideon in the Midianite War

And the children of Israel did that which was evil in the sight of the LORD, and the LORD delivered them into the hand of Midian seven years. And because of Midian the children of Israel made them the dens which are in the mountains, and the caves, and the strongholds. And so it was, when Israel had sown, that the Midianites came up, and the Amalekites, and the children of the east; and they encamped against them, and destroyed the increase of the earth, and left no sustenance in Israel, neither sheep, nor ox, nor ass. For they came up with their cattle and their tents, they came in as locusts for multitude; both they and their camels were without number. And Israel was brought very low because of Midian; and the children of Israel cried unto the LORD.

And the angel of the LORD came, and sat under the oak which was in Ophrah, that pertained unto Joash the Abi-ezrite: and his son Gideon was beating out wheat in the winepress, to hide it from the Midianites. And the angel

Gideon — **Bible Stories**

of the LORD appeared unto him, and said unto him, The LORD is with thee, thou mighty man of valour. And Gideon said unto him, Oh, my lord, if the LORD be with us, why then is all this befallen us? and where be all his wondrous works which our fathers told us of, saying, Did not the LORD bring us up from Egypt? but now the LORD hath cast us off, and delivered us into the hand of Midian. And the LORD looked upon him, and said, Go in this thy might, and save Israel from the hand of Midian: have not I sent thee? And he said unto him, Oh Lord, wherewith shall I save Israel? behold, my family is the poorest in Manasseh, and I am the least in my father's house. And the LORD said unto him, Surely I will be with thee, and thou shalt smite the Midianites as one man. And he said unto him, If now I have found grace in thy sight, then shew me a sign that it is thou that talkest with me. Depart not hence, I pray thee, until I come unto thee, and bring forth my present, and lay it before thee. And he said, I will tarry until thou come again. And Gideon went in, and made ready a kid, and unleavened cakes of meal: the flesh he put in a basket, and he put the broth in a pot, and brought it out unto him under the oak, and presented it. And the angel of God said unto him, Take the flesh and the unleavened cakes, and lay them upon this rock, and pour out the broth. And he did so. Then the angel of the LORD put forth the end of the staff that was in his hand, and touched the flesh and the unleavened cakes; and there went up fire out of the rock, and consumed the flesh and the unleavened cakes; and the angel of the LORD departed out of his sight. And Gideon saw that he was the angel of the LORD; and Gideon said, Alas, O Lord GOD! forasmuch as I have seen the angel of the LORD face to face. And the LORD said unto him, Peace be unto thee; fear not: thou shalt not die. Then Gideon built an altar there unto the LORD.

Then all the Midianites and the Amalekites and the children of the east assembled themselves together; and they passed over, and pitched in the valley of Jezreel. But the spirit of the LORD came upon Gideon; and he blew a trumpet; and Abiezer was gathered together after him. And he sent messengers throughout all Manasseh; and they also were gathered together after him: and he sent messengers unto Asher, and unto Zebulun, and unto Naphtali; and they came up to meet them. And Gideon said unto God, If thou wilt save Israel by mine hand, as thou hast spoken, behold, I will put a fleece of wool on the threshing-floor; if there be dew on the fleece only, and it be dry upon all the ground, then shall I know that thou wilt save Israel by mine hand, as thou hast spoken. And it was so: for he rose up early on the morrow, and pressed the fleece together, and wringed the dew out of the fleece, a bowlful of water. And Gideon said unto God, Let not thine anger be kindled against me, and I will speak but this once: let me prove, I pray thee, but this once with the fleece; let it now be dry only upon the fleece, and upon all the ground let there be dew. And God did so that night: for it was dry upon the fleece only, and there was dew on all the ground.

Then Gideon, and all the people that were with him, rose up early, and pitched beside the spring of Harod: and the camp of Midian was on the north side of them, in the valley.

And the LORD said unto Gideon, The people that are with thee are too many for me to give the Midianites into their hand, lest Israel vaunt themselves against me, saying, Mine own hand hath saved me. Now therefore go to, proclaim in the ears of the people, saying, Whosoever is fearful and trembling, let him return and depart from mount Gilead. And there returned of the people twenty and two thousand; and there remained ten thousand.

And the LORD said unto Gideon, The people are yet too many; bring them down unto the water, and I will try them for thee there: and it shall be, that of whom I say unto thee, This shall go with thee, the same shall go with thee; and of whomsoever I say unto thee, This shall not go with thee, the same shall not go. So he brought down the people unto the water: and the LORD said unto Gideon, Every one that lappeth of the water with his tongue, as a dog lappeth, him shalt thou set by himself; likewise every one that boweth down upon his knees to drink. And the number of them that lapped, putting their hand to their mouth, was three hundred men: but all the rest of the people bowed down upon their knees to drink water. And the LORD said unto Gideon, By the three hundred men that lapped will I save you, and deliver the Midianites into thine hand: and let all the people go every man unto his place. So the people took victuals in their hand, and their trumpets: and he sent all the men of Israel every man unto his tent, but retained the three hundred men. And the camp of Midian was beneath him in the valley.

And it came to pass the same night, that the LORD said unto him, Arise, get thee down into the camp; for I have delivered it into thine hand. But if thou fear to go down, go thou with Purah thy servant down to the camp: and thou shalt hear what they say; and afterward shall thine hands be strengthened to go down into the camp. Then went he down with Purah his servant unto the outermost part of the armed men that were in the camp. And the Midianites and the Amalekites and all the children of the east lay along in the valley like locusts for multitude; and their camels were without number, as the sand which is upon the sea shore for multitude. And when Gideon was come, behold, there was a man that told a dream unto his fellow, and said, Behold, I dreamed a dream, and, lo, a cake of barley bread tumbled into the camp of Midian, and came unto the tent, and smote it that it fell, and turned it upside down, that the tent lay along. And his fellow answered and said, This is nothing else save the sword of Gideon the son of Joash, a man of Israel: into his hand God hath delivered Midian, and all the host.

And it was so, when Gideon heard the telling of the dream, and the interpretation thereof, that he worshipped; and he returned into the camp of Israel, and said, Arise; for the LORD hath delivered into your hand the host of Midian. And he divided the three hundred men into three companies, and he put into the hands of all of them trumpets, and empty pitchers, with torches within the pitchers. And he said unto them, Look on me, and do likewise: and, behold, when I come to the outermost part of the camp, it shall be that, as I do, so shall ye do. When I blow the trumpet, I and all that are with me, then blow ye the trumpets also on every side of all the camp, and say, For the LORD and for Gideon.

So Gideon, and the hundred men that were with him, came unto the outermost part of the camp in the beginning of the middle watch, when they had but newly set the watch: and they blew the trumpets, and brake in pieces the pitchers that were in their hands. And the three companies blew the trumpets, and brake the pitchers, and held the torches in their left hands, and the trumpets in their right hands to blow withal: and they cried, The sword of the LORD and of Gideon. And they stood every man in his place round about the camp: and all the host ran; and they shouted, and put them to flight. And they blew the three hundred trumpets, and the LORD set every man's sword against his fellow, and against all the host: and the host fled. And Gideon took the two kings of Midian, Zebah and Zalmunna, and discomfited all the host.

Then the men of Israel said unto Gideon, Rule thou over us, both thou, and thy son, and thy son's son also: for thou hast saved us out of the hand of Midian. And Gideon said unto them, I will not rule over you, neither shall my son rule over you: the LORD shall rule over you.

So Midian was subdued before the children of Israel, and they lifted up their heads no more.

V

Jephthah's Vow

Now Jephthah the Gileadite was a mighty man of valour. And it came to pass that the children of Ammon made war against Israel. And it was so, that, when the children of Ammon made war against Israel, the elders of Gilead went to fetch Jephthah out of the land of Tob: and they said unto Jephthah, Come and be our chief, that we may fight with the children of Ammon. And Jephthah said unto the elders of Gilead, Did not ye hate me, and drive me out of my father's house? and why are ye come unto me now when ye are in distress? And the elders of Gilead said unto Jephthah, Therefore are we turned again to thee now, that thou mayest go with us, and fight with the children of Ammon, and thou shalt be our head over all the inhabitants of Gilead. And Jephthah said unto the elders of Gilead, If ye bring me home again to fight with the children of Ammon, and the LORD deliver them before me, shall I be your head? And the elders of Gilead said unto Jephthah, The LORD shall be witness between us; surely according to thy word so will we do. Then Jephthah went with the elders of Gilead, and the people made him head and chief over them.

Then the spirit of the LORD came upon Jephthah, and he passed over unto the children of Ammon. And Jephthah vowed a vow unto the LORD, and said, If thou wilt indeed deliver the children of Ammon into mine hand, then it shall be, that whatsoever cometh forth of the doors of my house to meet me, when I return in peace from the children of Ammon, it shall be the LORD'S, and I will offer it up for a burnt offering. So Jephthah passed over unto the children of Ammon to fight against them; and the LORD delivered them into his hand. And he smote them with a very great slaughter. So the children of Ammon were subdued before the children of Israel.

And Jephthah came to Mizpah unto his house, and, behold, his daughter came out to meet him with timbrels and with dances: and she was his only child; beside her he had neither son nor daughter. And it came to pass, when he saw her, that he rent his clothes, and said, Alas, my daughter! thou hast brought me very low, and thou art one of them that trouble me: for I have opened my mouth unto the LORD, and I cannot go back. And she said unto him, My father, thou hast opened thy mouth unto the LORD; do unto me according to that which hath proceeded out of thy mouth; forasmuch as the LORD hath taken vengeance for thee of thine enemies, even of the children of Ammon. And she said unto her father, Let this thing be done for me: let me alone two months, that I may depart and go down upon the mountains, and bewail my virginity, I and my companions. And he said, Go. And he sent her away for two months: and she departed, she and her companions, and bewailed her virginity upon the mountains. And it came to pass at the end of two months, that she returned unto her father, who did with her according to his vow which he had vowed. And it was a custom in Israel, that the daughters of Israel went yearly to celebrate the daughter of Jephthah the Gileadite four days in a year.

vi

Stories of Samson

Samson's Wedding Feast

And Samson went down to Timnah, and saw a woman in Timnah of the daughters of the Philistines. And he came up, and told his father and his mother, and said, I have seen a woman in Timnah of the daughters of the Philistines: now therefore get her for me to wife. Then his father and his mother said unto him, Is there never a woman among the daughters of thy brethren, or among all my people, that thou goest to take a wife of the Philistines? And Samson said unto his father, Get her for me; for she pleaseth me well. But his father and his mother knew not that it was of the LORD; for he sought an occasion against the Philistines. Now at that time the Philistines had rule over Israel. Then went Samson down, and his father and his mother, to Timnah, and came to the vineyards of Timnah: and, behold, a young lion roared against him. And the spirit of the LORD came mightily upon him, and he rent him as he would have rent a kid, and he had nothing in his hand: but he told not his father or his mother what he had done. And he went down and talked with the woman; and she pleased Samson well. And after a while he returned to take her, and he turned aside to see the carcase of the lion: and, behold, there was a swarm of bees in the body of the lion, and honey. And he took it into his hands, and went on, eating as he went, and he came to his father and mother, and gave unto them, and they did eat: but he told them not that he had taken the honey out of the body of the lion. And his father went down unto the woman: and Samson made there a feast: for so used the young men to do. And it came to pass, when they saw him, that they brought thirty companions to be with him. And Samson said unto them, Let me now put forth a riddle unto you: if ye can declare it me within the seven days of the feast, and find it out, then I will give you thirty linen garments and thirty changes of raiment: but if ye cannot declare it me, then shall ye give me thirty linen garments and thirty changes of raiment. And they said unto him, Put forth thy riddle, that we may hear it. And he said unto them,

> Out of the eater came forth meat,
> And out of the strong came forth sweetness.

And they could not in three days declare the riddle. And it came to pass on the seventh day, that they said unto Samson's wife, Entice thy husband, that he may declare unto us the riddle, lest we burn thee and thy father's house with fire: have ye called us to impoverish us? is it not so? And Samson's wife wept before him, and said, Thou dost but hate me, and lovest me not: thou hast put forth a riddle unto the children of my people, and hast not told it me. And he said unto her, Behold, I have not told it my father nor my mother, and shall I tell thee? And she wept before him the seven days, while their feast lasted: and it came to pass on the seventh day, that he told her, because she pressed him sore: and she told the riddle to the children of her people. And the men of the city said unto him on the seventh day before the sun went down:

> What is sweeter than honey?
> And what is stronger than a lion?

And he said unto them:

> If ye had not plowed with my heifer,
> Ye had not found out my riddle.

And the spirit of the LORD came mightily upon him, and he went down to Ashkelon, and smote thirty men of them, and took their spoil, and gave the changes of raiment unto them that declared the riddle. And his anger was kindled, and he went up to his father's house. But Samson's wife was given to his companion, whom he had used as his friend.

The Jawbone of an Ass

The Philistines went up, and pitched in Judah, and spread themselves in Lehi. And the men of Judah said,

Why are ye come up against us? And they said, To bind Samson are we come up, to do to him as he hath done to us. Then three thousand men of Judah went down to the cleft of the rock of Etam, and said to Samson, Knowest thou not that the Philistines are rulers over us? what then is this that thou hast done unto us? And he said unto them, As they did unto me, so have I done unto them. And they said unto him, We are come down to bind thee, that we may deliver thee into the hand of the Philistines. And Samson said unto them, Swear unto me, that ye will not fall upon me yourselves. And they spake unto him, saying, No; but we will bind thee fast, and deliver thee into their hand: but surely we will not kill thee. And they bound him with two new ropes, and brought him up from the rock. When he came unto Lehi, the Philistines shouted as they met him: and the spirit of the LORD came mightily upon him, and the ropes that were upon his arms became as flax that was burnt with fire, and his bands dropped from off his hands. And he found a new jawbone of an ass, and put forth his hand, and took it, and smote a thousand men therewith. And Samson said,

> With the jawbone of an ass, heaps upon heaps,
> With the jawbone of an ass have I smitten a thousand men.

Samson and Delilah

And it came to pass afterward, that he loved a woman in the valley of Sorek, whose name was Delilah. And the lords of the Philistines came up unto her, and said unto her, Entice him, and see wherein his great strength lieth, and by what means we may prevail against him, that we may bind him to afflict him: and we will give thee every one of us eleven hundred pieces of silver. And Delilah said to Samson, Tell me, I pray thee, wherein thy great strength lieth, and wherewith thou mightest be bound to afflict thee. And Samson said unto her, If they bind me with seven green withes that were never dried, then shall I become weak, and be as another man. Then the lords of the Philistines brought up to her seven green withes which had not been dried, and she bound him with them. Now she had liers in wait abiding in the inner chamber. And she said unto him, The Philistines be upon thee, Samson. And he brake the withes, as a string of tow is broken when it toucheth the fire. So his strength was not known. And Delilah said unto Samson, Behold, thou hast mocked me, and told me lies: now tell me, I pray thee, wherewith thou mightest be bound. And he said unto her, If they only bind me with new ropes wherewith no work hath been done, then shall I become weak, and be as another man. So Delilah took new ropes, and bound him therewith, and said unto him, The Philistines be upon thee, Samson.

And the liers in wait were abiding in the inner chamber. And he brake them from off his arms like a thread. And Delilah said unto Samson, Hitherto thou hast mocked me, and told me lies: tell me wherewith thou mightest be bound. And he said unto her, If thou weavest the seven locks of my head with the web. And she fastened it with the pin, and said unto him, The Philistines be upon thee, Samson. And he awaked out of his sleep, and plucked away the pin of the beam, and the web. And she said unto him, How canst thou say, I love thee, when thine heart is not with me? thou hast mocked me these three times, and hast not told me wherein thy great strength lieth. And it came to pass, when she pressed him daily with her words, and urged him, that his soul was vexed unto death. And he told her all his heart, and said unto her, There hath not come a razor upon mine head; for I have been a Nazirite unto God from my mother's womb: if I be shaven, then my strength will go from me, and I shall become weak, and be like any other man. And when Delilah saw that he had told her all his heart, she sent and called for the lords of the Philistines, saying, Come up this once, for he hath told me all his heart. Then the lords of the Philistines came up unto her, and brought the money in their hand. And she made him sleep upon her knees; and she called for a man, and shaved off the seven locks of his head; and she began to afflict him, and his strength went from him. And she said, The Philistines be upon thee, Samson. And he awoke out of his sleep, and said, I will go out as at other times, and shake myself. But he wist not that the LORD was departed from him. And the Philistines laid hold on him, and put out his eyes; and they brought him down to Gaza, and bound him with fetters of brass; and he did grind in the prison house. Howbeit the hair of his head began to grow again after he was shaven.

Death of Samson

And the lords of the Philistines gathered them together for to offer a great sacrifice unto Dagon their god, and to rejoice: for they said, Our god hath delivered Samson our enemy into our hand. And when the people saw him, they praised their god: for they said, Our god hath delivered into our hand our enemy, and the destroyer of our country, which hath slain many of us. And it came to pass, when their hearts were merry, that they said, Call for Samson, that he may make us sport. And they called for Samson out of the prison house; and he made sport before them: and they set him between the pillars. And Samson said unto the lad that held him by the hand, Suffer me that I may feel the pillars whereupon the house resteth, that I may lean upon them. Now the house was full of men and women; and all the lords of the Philistines were there; and there were upon the roof about three thousand men and women, that beheld while Samson made sport. And Samson called unto the LORD, and said, O Lord GOD, remember me, I pray thee, and strengthen me, I pray thee, only this once, O God, that I may be avenged of the Philistines for one of my two eyes. And Samson took hold of the two middle pillars upon which the house rested, and leaned upon them, the one with his right hand, and the other with his left. And Samson said, Let me die with the Philistines. And he bowed himself with all his might; and the house fell upon the lords, and upon all the people that were therein. So the dead which he slew at his death were more than they which he slew in his life. Then his brethren and all the house of his father came down, and took him, and brought him up, and buried him in the burying-place of Manoah his father.

vii

The Old Man Eli and the Child Samuel

Birth of Samuel

Now there was a certain man of the hill country of Ephraim, and he had two wives; the name of the one was Hannah, and the name of the other Peninnah: and Peninnah had children, but Hannah had no children.

And this man went up out of his city from year to year to worship and to sacrifice unto the LORD of hosts in Shiloh.

Now Eli the priest sat upon his seat by the door post of the temple of the LORD. And Hannah was in bitterness of soul, and prayed unto the LORD, and wept sore. And she vowed a vow, and said, O LORD of hosts, if thou wilt indeed look on the affliction of thine handmaid, and remember me, and not forget thine handmaid, but wilt give unto thine handmaid a man child, then I will give him unto the LORD all the days of his life, and there shall no razor come upon his head. And it came to pass, as she continued praying before the LORD, that Eli marked her mouth. Now Hannah, she spake in her heart; only her lips moved, but her voice was not heard: therefore Eli thought she had been drunken. And Eli said unto her, How long wilt thou be drunken? put away thy wine from thee. And Hannah answered and said, No, my lord, I am a woman of a sorrowful spirit: I have drunk neither wine nor strong drink, but I poured out my soul before the LORD. Count not thine handmaid for a daughter of Belial: for out of the abundance of my complaint and my provocation have I spoken hitherto. Then Eli answered and said, Go in peace: and the God of Israel grant thy petition that thou hast asked of him. And she said, Let thy servant find grace in thy sight. So the woman went her way, and did eat, and her countenance was no more sad.

And it came to pass, when the time was come about, that Hannah bare a son; and she called his name 'Samuel,' saying, Because I have 'asked him of the LORD.' And when she had weaned him, she took him up with her, with three bullocks, and one ephah of meal, and a bottle of wine, and brought him unto the house of the LORD in Shiloh. And they slew the bullock, and brought the child to Eli. And she said, Oh my lord, as thy soul liveth, my lord, I am the woman that stood by thee here, praying unto the LORD. For this child I prayed; and the LORD hath given me my petition which I asked of him: therefore I also have granted him to the LORD; as long as he liveth he is granted to the LORD. And he worshipped the LORD there.

The Child Samuel called to be a Prophet

And the child Samuel ministered unto the LORD before Eli. And the word of the LORD was precious in those days; there was no open vision. And it came to pass at that time, when Eli was laid down in his place, (now his eyes had begun to wax dim, that he could not see,) and the lamp of God was not yet gone out, and Samuel was laid down to sleep, in the temple of the LORD, where the ark of God was; that the LORD called Samuel: and he said, Here am I. And he ran unto Eli, and said, Here am I; for thou calledst me. And he said, I called not;

lie down again. And he went and lay down. And the
LORD called yet again, Samuel. And Samuel arose and
went to Eli, and said, Here am I; for thou calledst me.
And he answered, I called not, my son; lie down again.
Now Samuel did not yet know the LORD, neither was
the word of the LORD yet revealed unto him. And the
LORD called Samuel again the third time. And he arose
and went to Eli, and said, Here am I; for thou calledst
me. And Eli perceived that the LORD had called the
child. Therefore Eli said unto Samuel, Go, lie down:
and it shall be, if he call thee, that thou shalt say, Speak,
LORD; for thy servant heareth. So Samuel went and
lay down in his place. And the LORD came, and stood,
and called as at other times, Samuel, Samuel. Then
Samuel said, Speak; for thy servant heareth. And the
LORD said to Samuel, Behold, I will do a thing in Israel,
at which both the ears of every one that heareth it shall
tingle. In that day I will perform against Eli all that
I have spoken concerning his house, from the beginning
even unto the end. For I have told him that I will judge
his house for ever, for the iniquity which he knew, because his sons did bring a curse upon themselves, and
he restrained them not. And Samuel lay until the morning, and opened the doors of the house of the LORD.
And Samuel feared to shew Eli the vision. Then Eli
called Samuel, and said, Samuel, my son. And he said,
Here am I. And he said, What is the thing that the

LORD hath spoken unto thee? I pray thee hide it not from me: God do so to thee, and more also, if thou hide any thing from me of all the things that he spake unto thee. And Samuel told him every whit, and hid nothing from him. And he said, It is the LORD: let him do what seemeth him good.

And Samuel grew, and the LORD was with him, and did let none of his words fall to the ground. And all Israel from Dan even to Beer-sheba knew that Samuel was established to be a prophet of the LORD.

Loss of the Ark and Death of Eli

Now Israel went out against the Philistines to battle, and pitched beside Eben-ezer: and the Philistines pitched in Aphek. And the Philistines put themselves in array against Israel: and when they joined battle, Israel was smitten before the Philistines: and they slew of the army in the field about four thousand men. And when the people were come into the camp, the elders of Israel said, Wherefore hath the LORD smitten us today before the Philistines? Let us fetch the ark of the covenant of the LORD out of Shiloh unto us, that it may come among us, and save us out of the hand of our enemies. So the people sent to Shiloh, and they brought from thence the ark of the covenant of the LORD of hosts, which sitteth upon the cherubim: and the two sons of Eli, Hophni and

Phinehas, were there with the ark of the covenant of God. And when the ark of the covenant of the LORD came into the camp, all Israel shouted with a great shout, so that the earth rang again. And when the Philistines heard the noise of the shout, they said, What meaneth the noise of this great shout in the camp of the Hebrews? And they understood that the ark of the LORD was come into the camp. And the Philistines were afraid, for they said, God is come into the camp. And they said, Woe unto us! for there hath not been such a thing heretofore. Woe unto us! who shall deliver us out of the hand of these mighty gods? these are the gods that smote the Egyptians with all manner of plagues in the wilderness. Be strong, and quit yourselves like men, O ye Philistines, that ye be not servants unto the Hebrews, as they have been to you: quit yourselves like men, and fight. And the Philistines fought, and Israel was smitten, and they fled every man to his tent: and there was a very great slaughter; for there fell of Israel thirty thousand footmen. And the ark of God was taken; and the two sons of Eli, Hophni and Phinehas, were slain. And there ran a man of Benjamin out of the army, and came to Shiloh the same day with his clothes rent, and with earth upon his head. And when he came, lo, Eli sat upon his seat by the way side watching: for his heart trembled for the ark of God. And when the man came into the city, and told it, all the city cried out. And when Eli heard the noise of the crying, he said, What meaneth the noise of this tumult? And the man hasted, and came and told Eli. Now Eli was ninety and eight years old; and his eyes were set, that he could not see. And the man said unto Eli, I am he that came out of the army, and I fled today out of the army. And he said, How went the matter, my son? And he that brought the tidings answered and said, Israel is fled before the Philistines, and there hath been also a great slaughter among the people, and thy two sons also, Hophni and Phinehas, are dead, and the ark of God is taken. And it came to pass, when he made mention of the ark of God, that he fell from off his seat backward by the side of the gate, and his neck brake, and he died: for he was an old man, and heavy. And he had judged Israel forty years.

The Return of the Ark

Now the Philistines had taken the ark of God, and they brought it from Eben-ezer unto Ashdod. And the Philistines took the ark of God, and brought it into the house of Dagon, and set it by Dagon. And when they of Ashdod arose early on the morrow, behold, Dagon was fallen upon his face to the ground before the ark of the LORD. And they took Dagon, and set him in his place again. And when they arose early on the morrow morning, behold, Dagon was fallen upon his face to the ground before the ark of the LORD; and the head of Dagon and both the palms of his hands lay cut off upon the threshold; only the stump of Dagon was left to him. Therefore neither the priests of Dagon, nor any that come into Dagon's house, tread on the threshold of Dagon in Ashdod, unto this day.

But the hand of the LORD was heavy upon them of Ashdod, and he destroyed them, and smote them with tumours, even Ashdod and the borders thereof. And when the men of Ashdod saw that it was so, they said, The ark of the God of Israel shall not abide with us: for his hand is sore upon us, and upon Dagon our god. They sent therefore and gathered all the lords of the Philistines unto them, and said, What shall we do with the ark of the God of Israel? And they answered, Let the ark of the God of Israel be carried about unto Gath. And they carried the ark of the God of Israel about thither. And it was so, that, after they had carried it about, the hand of the LORD was against the city with a very great discomfiture: and he smote the men of the city, both small and great, and tumours brake out upon them. So they sent the ark of God to Ekron. And it came to pass, as the ark of God came to Ekron, that the Ekronites cried out, saying, They have brought about the ark of the God of Israel to us, to slay us and our people. They sent therefore and gathered together all the lords of the Philistines, and they said, Send away the ark of the God of Israel, and let it go again to its own place, that it slay us not, and our people; for there was a deadly discomfiture throughout all the city; the hand of God was very heavy there. And the men that died not were smitten with the tumours: and the cry of the city went up to heaven.

And the ark of the LORD was in the country of the Philistines seven months. And the Philistines called for the priests and the diviners, saying, What shall we do with the ark of the LORD? shew us wherewith we shall send it to its place. And they said, If ye send away the ark of the God of Israel, send it not empty; but in any wise return him a guilt offering: then ye shall be healed, and it shall be known to you why his hand is not removed from you. Then said they, What shall be the guilt offering which we shall return to him? And they said, Five golden tumours, and five golden mice, according to the number of the lords of the Philistines: for one plague was on you all, and on your lords. Wherefore, ye shall make images of your tumours, and images of your mice that mar the land; and ye shall give glory unto the God of Israel: peradventure he will lighten his hand from off you, and from off your gods, and from off your land. Wherefore then do ye harden your hearts, as the Egyptians and Pharaoh hardened their hearts? when he had wrought wonderfully among them, did they not let the people go, and they departed? Now therefore take and prepare you a new cart, and two milch kine, on which there hath come no yoke, and tie the kine to the cart, and bring their calves home from them: and take the ark of the LORD, and lay it upon the cart; and put the jewels of gold, which ye return him for a guilt offering, in a coffer by the side thereof; and send it away, that it may go. And see, if it goeth up by the way of its own border to Beth-shemesh, then he hath done us this great evil: but if not, then we shall know that it is not his hand that smote us; it was a chance that happened to us. And the men did so; and took two milch kine, and tied them to the cart, and shut up their calves at home: and they put the ark of the LORD upon the cart, and the coffer with the mice of gold and the images of their tumours. And the kine took the straight way by the way to Beth-shemesh; they went along the high way, lowing as they went, and turned not aside to the right hand or to the left; and the lords of the Philistines went after them unto the border of Beth-shemesh. And they of Beth-shemesh were reaping their wheat harvest in the valley: and they lifted up their eyes, and saw the ark, and rejoiced to see it. And the cart came into the field of Joshua the Beth-shemite, and stood there, where there was a great stone: and they clave the wood of the cart, and offered up the kine for a burnt offering unto the LORD. And the Levites took down the ark of the LORD, and the coffer that was with it, wherein the jewels of gold were, and put them on the great stone: and the men of Beth-shemesh offered burnt offerings and sacrificed sacrifices the same day unto the LORD. And when the five lords of the Philistines had seen it, they returned to Ekron the same day.

viii

The Anointing of Saul

And it came to pass, when Samuel was old, that he made his sons judges over Israel. And his sons walked not in his ways, but turned aside after lucre, and took bribes, and perverted judgement.

Then all the elders of Israel gathered themselves together, and came to Samuel unto Ramah: and they said unto him, Behold thou art old, and thy sons walk not in thy ways: now make us a king to judge us like all the nations. But the thing displeased Samuel, when they said, Give us a king to judge us. And Samuel prayed unto the LORD. And the LORD said unto Samuel, Hearken unto the voice of the people in all that they say unto thee: for they have not rejected thee, but they have rejected me, that I should not be king over them. According to all the works which they have done since the day that I brought them up out of Egypt even unto this day, in that they have forsaken me, and served other gods, so do they also unto thee. Now therefore hearken unto their voice: howbeit thou shalt protest solemnly unto them, and shalt shew them the manner of the king that shall reign over them.

And Samuel told all the words of the LORD unto the people that asked of him a king. And he said, This will be the manner of the king that shall reign over you: he will take your sons, and appoint them unto him, for his chariots, and to be his horsemen; and they shall run before his chariots: and he will appoint them unto him for captains of thousands, and captains of fifties; and he will set some to plough his ground, and to reap his harvest, and to make his instruments of war, and the instruments of his chariots. And he will take your daughters to be confectionaries, and to be cooks, and to be bakers. And he will take your fields, and your vineyards, and your oliveyards, even the best of them, and give them to his servants. And he will take the tenth of your seed, and of your vineyards, and give to his officers, and to his servants. And he will take your menservants, and your maidservants, and your goodliest young men, and your asses, and put them to his work. He will take the tenth of your flocks: and ye shall be his servants. And ye shall cry out in that day because of your king which ye shall have chosen you; and the LORD will not answer you in that day. But the people refused to hearken unto the voice of Samuel; and they said, Nay; but we will have a king over us; that we also may be like all the nations; and that our king may judge us, and go out before us, and fight our battles. And Samuel heard all the words of the people, and he rehearsed them in the ears of the LORD. And the LORD said to Samuel, Hearken unto their voice, and make them a king. And Samuel said unto the men of Israel, Go ye every man unto his city.

Now there was a man of Benjamin, whose name was Kish, a mighty man of valour. And he had a son, whose name was Saul, a young man and a goodly: and there was not among the children of Israel a goodlier person than he: from his shoulders and upward he was higher than any of the people. And the asses of Kish Saul's father were lost. And Kish said to Saul his son, Take now one of the servants with thee, and arise, go seek the asses. And he passed through the hill country of Ephraim, and passed through the land of Shalishah, but they found them not: then they passed through the land of Shaalim, and there they were not: and he passed through the land of the Benjamites, but they found them not. When they were come to the land of Zuph, Saul said to his servant that was with him, Come and let us return; lest my father leave caring for the asses, and take thought for us. And he said unto him, Behold now, there is in this city a man of God, and he is a man that is held in honour; all that he saith cometh surely to pass: now let us go thither; peradventure he can tell us concerning our journey whereon we go. Then said Saul to his servant, But, behold, if we go, what shall we bring the man? for the bread is spent in our vessels, and there is not a present to bring to the man of God: what have we? And the servant answered Saul again, and said, Behold, I have in my hand the fourth part of a shekel of silver: that will I give to the man of God, to tell us our way.

Then said Saul to his servant, Well said; come, let us go. So they went unto the city where the man of God was. As they went up the ascent to the city, they found young maidens going out to draw water, and said unto them, Is the seer here? And they answered them, and said, He is; behold, he is before thee: make haste now, for he is come today into the city; for the people have a sacrifice today in the high place: as soon as ye be come into the city, ye shall straightway find him, before he go up to the high place to eat: for the people will not eat until he come, because he doth bless the sacrifice; and afterwards they eat that be bidden. Now therefore get you up; for at this time ye shall find him. And they went up to the city; and as they came within the city, behold, Samuel came out against them, for to go up to the high place.

Now the LORD had revealed unto Samuel a day before Saul came, saying, Tomorrow about this time I will send thee a man out of the land of Benjamin, and thou shalt anoint him to be prince over my people Israel, and he shall save my people out of the hand of the Philistines: for I have looked upon my people, because their cry is come unto me. And when Samuel saw Saul, the LORD said unto him, Behold the man of whom I spake to thee! this same shall have authority over my people. Then Saul drew near to Samuel in the gate, and said, Tell me, I pray thee, where the seer's house is. And Samuel answered Saul, and said, I am the seer; go up before me unto the high place, for ye shall eat with me today: and in the morning I will let thee go, and will tell thee all that is in thine heart. And as for thine asses that were lost three days ago, set not thy mind on them; for they are found. And on whom is all the desire of Israel? Is it not on thee, and on all thy father's house? And Saul answered and said, Am not I a Benjamite, of the smallest of the tribes of Israel? and my family the least of all the families of the tribe of Benjamin? wherefore then speakest thou to me after this manner? And Samuel took Saul and his servant, and brought them into the guest-chamber, and made them sit in the chiefest place among them that were bidden, which were about thirty persons. And Samuel said unto the cook, Bring the portion which I gave thee, of which I said unto thee, Set it by thee. And the cook took up the thigh, and that which was upon it, and set it before Saul. And Samuel said, Behold that which hath been reserved! set it before thee and eat; because unto the appointed time hath it been kept for thee, for I said, I have invited the people. So Saul did eat with Samuel that day. And when they were come down from the high place into the city, he communed with Saul upon the housetop. And they arose early: and it came to pass about the spring of the day, that Samuel called to Saul on the housetop, saying, Up, that I may send thee away. And Saul arose, and they went out both of them, he and Samuel, abroad. As they were going down at the end of the city, Samuel said to Saul, Bid the servant pass on before us, (and he passed on,) but stand thou still at this time, that I may cause thee to hear the word of God. Then Samuel took the vial of oil, and poured it upon his head, and kissed him, and said, Is it not that the LORD hath anointed thee to be prince over his inheritance? When thou art departed from me today, then thou shalt find two men by Rachel's sepulchre, and they will say unto thee, The asses which thou wentest to seek are found: and, lo, thy father hath left the care of the asses, and taketh thought for you, saying, What shall I do for my son? Then shalt thou go on forward from thence, and thou shalt come to the oak of Tabor, and there shall meet thee there three men going up to God to Beth-el, one carrying three kids, and another carrying three loaves of bread, and another carrying a bottle of wine: and they will salute thee, and give thee two loaves of bread; which thou shalt receive of their hand. After that thou shalt come to the hill of God, where is the garrison of the

Philistines: and it shall come to pass, when thou art come thither to the city, that thou shalt meet a band of prophets coming down from the high place with a psaltery, and a timbrel, and a pipe, and a harp, before them; and they shall be prophesying: and the spirit of the LORD will come mightily upon thee, and thou shalt prophesy with them, and shalt be turned into another man. And let it be, when these signs are come unto thee, that thou do as occasion serve thee; for God is with thee. And thou shalt go down before me to Gilgal; and, behold, I will come down unto thee, to offer burnt offerings, and to sacrifice sacrifices of peace offerings: seven days shalt thou tarry, till I come unto thee, and shew thee what thou shalt do. And it was so, that when he had turned his back to go from Samuel, God gave him another heart: and all those signs came to pass that day.

And when they came thither to the hill, behold, a band of prophets met him; and the spirit of God came mightily upon him, and he prophesied among them. And it came to pass, when all that knew him beforetimes saw that, behold, he prophesied with the prophets, then the people said one to another, What is this that is come unto the son of Kish? Is Saul also among the prophets? Therefore it became a proverb, Is Saul also among the prophets? And when he had made an end of prophesying, he came to the high place.

And Saul's uncle said unto him and to his servant,

Whither went ye? And he said, To seek the asses: and when we saw that they were not found, we came to Samuel. And Saul's uncle said, Tell me, I pray thee, what Samuel said unto you. And Saul said unto his uncle, He told us plainly that the asses were found. But concerning the matter of the kingdom, whereof Samuel spake, he told him not.

And Samuel called the people together unto the LORD to Mizpah; and he said unto the children of Israel, Thus saith the LORD, the God of Israel, I brought up Israel out of Egypt, and I delivered you out of the hand of the Egyptians, and out of the hand of all the kingdoms that oppressed you: but ye have this day rejected your God, who himself saveth you out of all your calamities and your distresses; and ye have said unto him, Nay, but set a king over us. Now therefore present yourselves before the LORD by your tribes, and by your thousands. So Samuel brought all the tribes of Israel near, and the tribe of Benjamin was taken. And he brought the tribe of Benjamin near by their families, and the family of the Matrites was taken: and Saul the son of Kish was taken; but when they sought him, he could not be found. Therefore they asked of the LORD further, Is there yet a man to come hither? And the LORD answered, Behold, he hath hid himself among the stuff. And they ran and fetched him thence; and when he stood among the people, he was higher than any of the people from his shoulders and upward. And Samuel said to all the people, See ye him whom the LORD hath chosen, that there is none like him among all the people? And all the people shouted, and said, God save the king.

Then Samuel told the people the manner of the kingdom, and wrote it in a book, and laid it up before the LORD. And Samuel sent all the people away, every man to his house.

ix

The Rejection of Saul and Anointing of David

And Samuel said unto Saul, The LORD sent me to anoint thee to be king over his people, over Israel: now therefore hearken thou unto the voice of the words of the LORD. Thus saith the LORD of hosts, I have marked that which Amalek did to Israel, how he set himself against him in the way, when he came up out of Egypt. Now go and smite Amalek, and utterly destroy all that they have, and spare them not; but slay both man and woman, infant and suckling, ox and sheep, camel and ass.

And Saul smote the Amalekites. And he took Agag the king of the Amalekites alive, and utterly destroyed all the people with the edge of the sword. But Saul and the people spared Agag, and the best of the sheep, and of the oxen, and of the fatlings, and the lambs, and all that was good, and would not utterly destroy them: but every thing that was vile and refuse, that they destroyed utterly.

Then came the word of the LORD unto Samuel, saying, It repenteth me that I have set up Saul to be king: for he is turned back from following me, and hath not performed my commandments. And Samuel was wroth; and he cried unto the LORD all night. And Samuel rose early to meet Saul in the morning; and it was told Samuel, saying, Saul came to Carmel, and, behold, he set him up a monument, and is gone about, and passed on, and gone down to Gilgal. And Samuel came to Saul: and Saul said unto him, Blessed be thou of the LORD: I have performed the commandment of the LORD. And Samuel said, What meaneth then this bleating of the sheep in mine ears, and the lowing of the oxen which I hear? And Saul said, They have brought them from the Amalekites: for the people spared the best of the sheep and of the oxen, to sacrifice unto the LORD thy God; and the rest we have utterly destroyed. Then Samuel said unto Saul, Stay, and I will tell thee what the LORD hath said to me this night. And he said unto him, Say on. And Samuel said, Though thou wast little in thine own sight, wast thou not made the head of the tribes of Israel? And the LORD anointed thee king over Israel; and the LORD sent thee on a journey, and said, Go and utterly destroy the sinners the Amalekites, and fight against them until they be consumed. Wherefore then didst thou not obey the voice of the LORD, but didst fly upon the spoil, and didst that which was evil in the sight of the LORD? And Saul said unto Samuel, Yea, I have obeyed the voice of the LORD, and have gone the way which the LORD sent me, and have brought Agag the king of Amalek, and have utterly destroyed the Amalekites. But the people took of the spoil, sheep and oxen, the chief of the devoted things, to sacrifice unto the LORD thy God in Gilgal. And Samuel said, Hath the LORD as great delight in burnt offerings and sacrifices, as in obeying the voice of the LORD? Behold, to obey is better than sacrifice, and to hearken than the fat of rams. Because thou hast rejected the word of the LORD, he hath also rejected thee from being king. And Saul said unto Samuel, I have sinned: for I have transgressed the commandment of the LORD, and thy words: because I feared the people, and obeyed their voice. Now therefore, I pray thee, pardon my sin, and turn again with me, that I may worship the LORD. And Samuel said unto Saul, I will not return with thee: for thou hast rejected the word of the LORD, and the LORD hath rejected thee from being king over Israel. And as Samuel turned about to go away, he laid hold upon the skirt of his robe, and it rent. And Samuel said unto him, The LORD hath rent the kingdom of Israel from thee this day, and hath given it to a neighbour of thine, that is better than thou. And also the Strength of Israel will not lie nor repent: for he is not a man, that he should repent. Then he said, I have sinned: yet honour me now, I pray thee, before the elders of my people, and before Israel, and turn again with me, that I may worship the LORD thy God. So Samuel turned again after Saul; and Saul worshipped the LORD.

Then said Samuel, Bring ye hither to me Agag the king of the Amalekites. And Agag came unto him delicately. And Agag said, Surely the bitterness of death is past. And Samuel said, As thy sword hath made women childless, so shall thy mother be childless among women. And Samuel hewed Agag in pieces before the LORD in Gilgal.

Then Samuel went to Ramah; and Saul went up to his house to Gibeah of Saul. And Samuel came no more to see Saul until the day of his death; for Samuel mourned for Saul: and the LORD repented that he had made Saul king over Israel.

And the LORD said unto Samuel, How long wilt thou mourn for Saul, seeing I have rejected him from being king over Israel? fill thine horn with oil, and go, I will send thee to Jesse the Beth-lehemite: for I have provided me a king among his sons. And Samuel said, How can I go? if Saul hear it, he will kill me. And the LORD said, Take an heifer with thee, and say, I am come to sacrifice to the LORD. And call Jesse to the sacrifice, and I will shew thee what thou shalt do: and thou shalt anoint unto me him whom I name unto thee. And Samuel did that which the LORD spake, and came to Beth-lehem. And the elders of the city came to meet him trembling, and said, Comest thou peaceably? And he said, Peaceably: I am come to sacrifice unto the LORD: sanctify yourselves, and come with me to the sacrifice. And he sanctified Jesse and his sons, and called them to the sacrifice. And it came to pass, when they were come, that he looked on Eliab, and said, Surely the LORD'S anointed is before him. But the LORD said unto Samuel, Look not on his countenance, or on the height of his stature; because I have rejected him: for the LORD seeth not as man seeth; for man looketh on the outward appearance, but the LORD looketh on the heart. Then Jesse called Abinadab, and made him pass before Samuel. And he said, Neither hath the LORD chosen this. Then Jesse made Shammah to pass by. And he said, Neither hath the LORD chosen this. And Jesse made seven of his sons to pass before Samuel. And Samuel said unto Jesse, The LORD hath not chosen these. And Samuel said unto Jesse, Are here all thy children? And he said, There remaineth yet the youngest, and, behold, he keepeth the sheep. And Samuel said unto Jesse, Send and fetch him: for we will not sit down till he come hither. And he sent, and brought him in. Now he was ruddy, and withal of a beautiful countenance, and goodly to look upon. And the LORD said, Arise, anoint him: for this is he. Then Samuel took the horn of oil, and anointed him in the midst of his brethren: and the spirit of the LORD came mightily upon David from that day forward. So Samuel rose up, and went to Ramah.

X

The Feud of Saul and David and the Friendship of David and Jonathan

David and Goliath

Now the Philistines gathered together their armies to battle, and Saul and the men of Israel were gathered together, and set the battle in array against the Philistines. And the Philistines stood on the mountain on the one side, and Israel stood on the mountain on the other side: and there was a valley between them. And there went out a champion out of the camp of the Philistines, named Goliath, of Gath, whose height was six cubits and a span. And he had an helmet of brass upon his head, and he was clad with a coat of mail; and the weight of the coat was five thousand shekels of brass. And he had greaves of brass upon his legs, and a javelin of brass between his shoulders. And the staff of his spear was like a weaver's beam; and his spear's head weighed six hundred shekels of iron: and his shieldbearer went before him. And he stood and cried unto the armies of Israel, and said unto

The Judges   David

them, Why are ye come out to set your battle in array? am not I a Philistine, and ye servants to Saul? choose you a man for you, and let him come down to me. If he be able to fight with me, and kill me, then will we be your servants: but if I prevail against him, and kill him, then shall ye be our servants, and serve us. And the Philistine said, I defy the armies of Israel this day; give me a man, that we may fight together. And when Saul and all Israel heard those words of the Philistine, they were dismayed, and greatly afraid.

Now David was the son of Jesse: and he had eight sons, and the three eldest sons of Jesse had gone after Saul to the battle, and David was the youngest. And the Philistine drew near morning and evening, and presented himself forty days.

And Jesse said unto David his son, Take now for thy brethren an ephah of this parched corn, and these ten loaves, and carry them quickly to the camp to thy brethren; and bring these ten cheeses unto the captain of their thousand, and look how thy brethren fare, and take their pledge. Now Saul, and they, and all the men of Israel, were in the vale of Elah, fighting with the Philistines. And David rose up early in the morning, and left the sheep with a keeper, and took, and went, as Jesse had commanded him; and he came to the place of the wagons, as the host which was going forth to the fight shouted for the battle. And Israel and the Philistines put the battle in array, army against army. And David left his baggage in the hand of the keeper of the baggage, and ran to the army, and came and saluted his brethren. And as he talked with them, behold, there came up the champion, the Philistine of Gath, Goliath by name, out of the ranks of the Philistines, and spake according to the same words: and David heard them. And all the men of Israel, when they saw the man, fled from him, and were sore afraid. And the men of Israel said, Have ye seen this man that is come up? surely to defy Israel is he come up: and it shall be, that the man who killeth him, the king will enrich him with great riches, and will give him his daughter, and make his father's house free in Israel. And David spake to the men that stood by him, saying, What shall be done to the man that killeth this Philistine, and taketh away the reproach from Israel? for who is this Philistine, that he should defy the armies of the living God? And the people answered him after this manner, saying, So shall it be done to the man that killeth him. And Eliab his eldest brother heard when he spake unto the men; and Eliab's anger was kindled against David, and he said, Why art thou come down? and with whom hast thou left those few sheep in the wilderness? I know thy pride, and the naughtiness of thine heart; for thou art come down that thou mightest see the battle. And David said, What have I now done? Is there not a cause? And he turned away from him toward another, and spake after the same manner: and the people answered him again after the former manner. And when the words were heard which David spake, they rehearsed them before Saul; and he sent for him. And David said to Saul, Let no man's heart fail because of him; thy servant will go and fight with this Philistine. And Saul said to David, Thou art not able to go against this Philistine to fight with him: for thou art but a youth, and he a man of war from his youth. And David said unto Saul, Thy servant kept his father's sheep; and when there came a lion, or a bear, and took a lamb out of the flock, I went out after him, and smote him, and delivered it out of his mouth: and when he arose against me, I caught him by his beard, and smote him, and slew him. Thy servant smote both the lion and the bear: and this Philistine shall be as one of them, seeing he hath defied the armies of the living God. And David said, The LORD that delivered me out of the paw of the lion, and out of the paw of the bear, he will deliver me out of the hand of this Philistine. And Saul said unto David, Go, and the LORD shall be with thee. And Saul clad David with his apparel, and he put an helmet of brass upon his head, and he clad him with a coat of mail. And David girded his sword upon his apparel, and he assayed to go; for he had not proved it. And David said unto Saul, I cannot go with these; for I have not proved them. And David put them off him. And he took his staff in his hand, and chose him five smooth stones out of the brook, and put them in the shepherd's bag which he had, even in his scrip; and his sling was in his hand: and he drew near to the Philistine.

And the Philistine came on and drew near unto David; and the man that bare the shield went before him. And when the Philistine looked about, and saw David, he disdained him: for he was but a youth, and ruddy, and withal of a fair countenance. And the Philistine said unto David, Am I a dog, that thou comest to me with staves? And the Philistine cursed David by his gods. And the Philistine said to David, Come to me, and I will give thy flesh unto the fowls of the air, and to the beasts of the field. Then said David to the Philistine, Thou comest to me with a sword, and with a spear, and with a javelin: but I come to thee in the name of the LORD of hosts, the God of the armies of Israel, which thou hast defied. This day will the LORD deliver thee into mine hand; and I will smite thee, and take thine head from off thee; and I will give the carcases of the host of the Philistines this day unto the fowls of the air, and to the wild beasts of the earth; that all the earth may know that there is a God in Israel; and that all this assembly may know that the LORD saveth not with sword and spear: for the battle is the LORD's, and he will give you into our hand. And it came to pass, when the Philistine arose, and came and drew nigh to meet David, that David hastened, and ran toward the army to meet the Philistine. And David put his hand in his bag, and took thence a stone, and slang it, and smote the Philistine in his forehead; and the stone sank into his forehead, and he fell upon his face to the earth. So David prevailed over the Philistine with a sling and with a stone, and smote the Philistine, and slew him; but there was no sword in the hand of David. Then David ran, and stood over the Philistine, and took his sword, and drew it out of the sheath thereof, and slew him, and cut off his head therewith. And when the Philistines saw that their champion was dead, they fled. And the men of Israel and of Judah arose, and shouted, and pursued the Philistines. And the children of Israel returned from chasing after the Philistines, and they spoiled their camp. And David took the head of the Philistine, and brought it to Jerusalem; but he put his armour in his tent.

How the Feud and the Friendship began

And when Saul saw David go forth against the Philistine, he said unto Abner, the captain of the host, Abner, whose son is this youth? And Abner said, As thy soul liveth, O king, I cannot tell. And the king said, Inquire thou whose son the stripling is. And as David returned from the slaughter of the Philistine, Abner took him, and brought him before Saul with the head of the Philistine in his hand. And Saul said to him, Whose son art thou, thou young man? And David answered, I am the son of thy servant

Jesse the Beth-lehemite. And it came to pass, when he had made an end of speaking unto Saul, that the soul of Jonathan was knit with the soul of David, and Jonathan loved him as his own soul. And Saul took him that day, and would let him go no more home to his father's house. Then Jonathan and David made a covenant, because he loved him as his own soul. And Jonathan stripped himself of the robe that was upon him, and gave it to David, and his apparel, even to his sword, and to his bow, and to his girdle. And David went out whithersoever Saul sent him, and behaved himself wisely: and Saul set him over the men of war, and it was good in the sight of all the people, and also in the sight of Saul's servants.

And it came to pass as they came, when David returned from the slaughter of the Philistine, that the women came out of all the cities of Israel, singing and dancing, to meet king Saul, with timbrels, with joy, and with instruments of music. And the women sang one to another in their play, and said,

>   Saul hath slain his thousands,
>   And David his ten thousands.

And Saul was very wroth, and this saying displeased him; and he said, They have ascribed unto David ten thousands, and to me they have ascribed but thousands: and what can he have more but the kingdom? And Saul eyed David from that day and forward.

The Judges &- David

And it came to pass on the morrow, that an evil spirit from God came mightily upon Saul, and he prophesied in the midst of the house: and David played with his hand, as he did day by day: and Saul had his spear in his hand. And Saul cast the spear; for he said, I will smite David even to the wall. And David avoided out of his presence twice. And Saul was afraid of David, because the LORD was with him, and was departed from Saul. Therefore Saul removed him from him, and made him his captain over a thousand; and he went out and came in before the people. And David behaved himself wisely in all his ways; and the LORD was with him. And when Saul saw that he behaved himself very wisely, he stood in awe of him. But all Israel and Judah loved David; for he went out and came in before them.

The Escape by Night

And Saul spake to Jonathan his son, and to all his servants, that they should slay David. But Jonathan Saul's son delighted much in David. And Jonathan told David, saying, Saul my father seeketh to slay thee: now therefore, I pray thee, take heed to thyself in the morning, and abide in a secret place, and hide thyself: and I will go out and stand beside my father in the field where thou art, and I will commune with my father of thee; and if I see aught, I will tell thee. And Jonathan spake good of David unto

Saul his father, and said unto him, Let not the king sin against his servant, against David; because he hath not sinned against thee, and because his works have been to thee-ward very good: for he put his life in his hand, and smote the Philistine, and the LORD wrought a great victory for all Israel: thou sawest it, and didst rejoice: wherefore then wilt thou sin against innocent blood, to slay David without a cause? And Saul hearkened unto the voice of Jonathan: and Saul sware, As the LORD liveth, he shall not be put to death. And Jonathan called David, and Jonathan shewed him all those things. And Jonathan brought David to Saul, and he was in his presence, as beforetime.

And there was war again: and David went out, and fought with the Philistines, and slew them with a great slaughter; and they fled before him. And an evil spirit from the LORD was upon Saul, as he sat in his house with his spear in his hand; and David played with his hand. And Saul sought to smite David even to the wall with the spear; but he slipped away out of Saul's presence, and he smote the spear into the wall: and David fled, and escaped that night. And Saul sent messengers unto David's house, to watch him, and to slay him in the morning: and Michal David's wife told him, saying, If thou save not thy life tonight, tomorrow thou shalt be slain. So Michal let David down through the window: and he went, and fled, and escaped. And Michal took the teraphim, and laid it in the bed, and put a pillow of goats' hair at the head thereof, and covered it with the clothes. And when Saul sent messengers to take David, she said, He is sick. And Saul sent the messengers to see David, saying, Bring him up to me in the bed, that I may slay him. And when the messengers came in, behold, the teraphim was in the bed, with the pillow of goats' hair at the head thereof. And Saul said unto Michal, Why hast thou deceived me thus, and let mine enemy go, that he is escaped? And Michal answered Saul, He said unto me, Let me go; why should I kill thee?

The Secret Meeting of David and Jonathan

And David came and said before Jonathan, What have I done? what is mine iniquity? and what is my sin before thy father, that he seeketh my life? And he said unto him, God forbid; thou shalt not die: behold, my father doeth nothing either great or small, but that he discloseth it unto me: and why should my father hide this thing from me? it is not so. And David sware moreover, and said, Thy father knoweth well that I have found grace in thine eyes; and he saith, Let not Jonathan know this, lest he be grieved: but truly as the LORD liveth, and as thy soul liveth, there is but a step between me and death. Then said Jonathan unto David, Whatsoever thy soul desireth, I will even do it for thee. And David said unto Jonathan,

Behold, tomorrow is the new moon, and I should not fail to sit with the king at meat: but let me go that I may hide myself in the field unto the third day at even. If thy father miss me at all, then say, David earnestly asked leave of me that he might run to Beth-lehem his city: for it is the yearly sacrifice there for all the family. If he say thus, It is well; thy servant shall have peace: but if he be wroth, then know that evil is determined by him. Therefore deal kindly with thy servant; for thou hast brought thy servant into a covenant of the LORD with thee: but if there be in me iniquity, slay me thyself; for why shouldest thou bring me to thy father? And Jonathan said, Far be it from thee: for if I should at all know that evil were determined by my father to come upon thee, then would not I tell it thee? Then said David to Jonathan, Who shall tell me if perchance thy father answer thee roughly? And Jonathan said unto David, Come and let us go out into the field. And they went out both of them into the field.

And Jonathan said unto David, The LORD, the God of Israel, be witness; when I have sounded my father about this time tomorrow, or the third day, behold, if there be good toward David, shall I not then send unto thee, and disclose it unto thee? The LORD do so to Jonathan, and more also, should it please my father to do thee evil, if I disclose it not unto thee, and send thee away, that thou mayest go in peace: and the LORD be with thee, as he hath been with my father. And thou shalt not only while yet I live shew me the kindness of the LORD, that I die not: but also thou shalt not cut off thy kindness from my house for ever: no, not when the LORD hath cut off the enemies of David every one from the face of the earth. So Jonathan made a covenant with the house of David, saying, And the LORD shall require it at the hand of David's enemies. And Jonathan caused David to swear again, for the love that he had to him: for he loved him as he loved his own soul. Then Jonathan said unto him, Tomorrow is the new moon: and thou shalt be missed, because thy seat will be empty. And when thou hast stayed three days, thou shalt go down quickly, and come to the place where thou didst hide thyself when the business was in hand, and shalt remain by the stone Ezel. And I will shoot three arrows on the side thereof, as though I shot at a mark. And, behold, I will send the lad, saying, Go, find the arrows. If I say unto the lad, Behold, the arrows are on this side of thee: take them, and come; for there is peace to thee and no hurt, as the LORD liveth. But if I say thus unto the boy, Behold, the arrows are beyond thee: go thy way; for the LORD hath sent thee away. And as touching the matter which thou and I have spoken of, behold, the LORD is between thee and me for ever.

So David hid himself in the field: and when the new moon was come, the king sat him down to eat meat. And the king sat upon his seat, as at other times, even upon the seat by the wall; and Jonathan stood up, and

Abner sat by Saul's side: but David's place was empty. Nevertheless Saul spake not any thing that day: for he thought, Something hath befallen him. And it came to pass on the morrow after the new moon, which was the second day, that David's place was empty: and Saul said unto Jonathan his son, Wherefore cometh not the son of Jesse to meat, neither yesterday, nor today? And Jonathan answered Saul, David earnestly asked leave of me to go to Beth-lehem: and he said, Let me go, I pray thee; for our family hath a sacrifice in the city; and my brother, he hath commanded me to be there: and now, if I have found favour in thine eyes, let me get away, I pray thee, and see my brethren. Therefore he is not come unto the king's table. Then Saul's anger was kindled against Jonathan, and he said unto him, Thou son of a perverse rebellious woman, do not I know that thou hast chosen the son of Jesse to thine own shame? For as long as the son of Jesse liveth upon the ground, thou shalt not be stablished, nor thy kingdom. Wherefore now send and fetch him unto me, for he shall surely die. And Jonathan answered Saul his father, and said unto him, Wherefore should he be put to death? what hath he done? And Saul cast his spear at him to smite him: whereby Jonathan knew that it was determined of his father to put David to death. So Jonathan arose from the table in fierce anger, and did eat no meat the second day of the month: for he was grieved for David, because his father had done him shame.

And it came to pass in the morning, that Jonathan went out into the field at the time appointed with David, and a little lad with him. And he said unto his lad, Run, find now the arrows which I shoot. And as the lad ran, he shot an arrow beyond him. And when the lad was come to the place of the arrow which Jonathan had shot, Jonathan cried after the lad, and said, Is not the arrow beyond thee? And Jonathan cried after the lad, Make speed, haste, stay not. And Jonathan's lad gathered up the arrows, and came to his master. But the lad knew not any thing: only Jonathan and David knew the matter. And Jonathan gave his weapons unto his lad, and said unto him, Go, carry them to the city. And as soon as the lad was gone, David arose out of a place toward the South, and fell on his face to the ground, and bowed himself three times: and they kissed one another, and wept one with another, until David exceeded. And Jonathan said to David, Go in peace, forasmuch as we have sworn both of us in the name of the LORD, saying, The LORD shall be between me and thee, and between my seed and thy seed, for ever. And he arose and departed: and Jonathan went into the city.

The Adventure of the Spear and Water-cruse

And the Ziphites came unto Saul to Gibeah, saying, Doth not David hide himself in the hill of Hachilah, which is before the desert? Then Saul arose, and went down to the wilderness of Ziph, having three thousand chosen men of Israel with him, to seek David in the wilderness of Ziph. And Saul pitched in the hill of Hachilah, which is before the desert, by the way. But David abode in the wilderness, and he saw that Saul came after him into the wilderness. David therefore sent out spies, and understood that Saul was come of a certainty. And David arose, and came to the place where Saul had pitched: and David beheld the place where Saul lay, and Abner the son of Ner, the captain of his host: and Saul lay within the place of the wagons, and the people pitched round about him. Then answered David and said, Who will go down with me to Saul to the camp? And Abishai said, I will go down with thee. So David and Abishai came to the people by night: and, behold, Saul lay sleeping within the place of the wagons, with his spear stuck in the ground at his head: and Abner and the people lay round about him. Then said Abishai to David, God hath delivered up thine enemy into thine hand this day: now therefore let me smite him, I pray thee, with the spear to the earth at one stroke, and I will not smite him the second time. And David said to Abishai, Destroy him not: for who can put forth his hand against the LORD's anointed, and be guiltless? And David said, As the LORD liveth, the LORD shall smite him; or his day shall come to die; or he shall go down into battle, and perish. The

LORD forbid that I should put forth mine hand against the LORD's anointed: but now take, I pray thee, the spear that is at his head, and the cruse of water, and let us go. So David took the spear and the cruse of water from Saul's head; and they gat them away, and no man saw it, nor knew it, neither did any awake: for they were all asleep; because a deep sleep from the LORD was fallen upon them.

Then David went over to the other side, and stood on the top of the mountain afar off; a great space being between them: and David cried to the people, and to Abner the son of Ner, saying, Answerest thou not, Abner? Then Abner answered and said, Who art thou that criest to the king? And David said to Abner, Art not thou a valiant man? and who is like to thee in Israel? wherefore then hast thou not kept watch over thy lord the king? for there came one of the people in to destroy the king thy lord. This thing is not good that thou hast done. As the LORD liveth, ye are worthy to die, because ye have not kept watch over your lord, the LORD's anointed. And now, see, where the king's spear is, and the cruse of water that was at his head. And Saul knew David's voice, and said, Is this thy voice, my son David? And David said, It is my voice, my lord, O king. And he said, Wherefore doth my lord pursue after his servant? for what have I done? or what evil is in mine hand? Now therefore, I pray thee, let my lord the king hear the words of his servant. If it be the L ORD that hath stirred thee up against me, let him accept an offering: but if it be the children of men, cursed be they before the L ORD ; for they have driven me out this day that I should not cleave unto the inheritance of the L ORD , saying, Go, serve other gods. Now therefore, let not my blood fall to the earth away from the presence of the L ORD : for the king of Israel is come out to seek a flea, as when one doth hunt a partridge in the mountains. Then said Saul, I have sinned: return, my son David: for I will no more do thee harm, because my life was precious in thine eyes this day: behold, I have played the fool, and have erred exceedingly. And David answered and said, Behold the spear, O king! let then one of the young men come over and fetch it. And the L ORD shall render to every man his righteousness and his faithfulness: forasmuch as the L ORD delivered thee into my hand today, and I would not put forth mine hand against the L ORD 's anointed. And, behold, as thy life was much set by this day in mine eyes, so let my life be much set by in the eyes of the L ORD , and let him deliver me out of all tribulation. Then Saul said to David, Blessed be thou, my son David: thou shalt both do mightily, and shalt surely prevail. So David went his way, and Saul returned to his place.

The Judges & David

The Battle of Gilboa

Now the Philistines fought against Israel: and the men of Israel fled from before the Philistines, and fell down slain in mount Gilboa. And the Philistines followed hard upon Saul and upon his sons; and the Philistines slew the sons of Saul. And the battle went sore against Saul, and the archers overtook him; and he was greatly distressed by reason of the archers. Then said Saul to his armourbearer, Draw thy sword, and thrust me through therewith; lest these come and thrust me through, and abuse me. But his armourbearer would not; for he was sore afraid. Therefore Saul took his sword, and fell upon it. And when his armourbearer saw that Saul was dead, he likewise fell upon his sword, and died with him. So Saul died, and his three sons, and his armourbearer, and all his men, that same day together.

And it came to pass on the third day, that, behold, a man came out of the camp from Saul with his clothes rent, and earth upon his head: and so it was, when he came to David, that he fell to the earth, and did obeisance. And David said unto him, From whence comest thou? And he said unto him, Out of the camp of Israel am I escaped. And David said unto him, How went the matter? I pray thee, tell me. And he answered, The people are fled from the battle, and many of the people also are fallen and dead; and Saul and Jonathan his son are dead also. And David said unto the young man that told him, How knowest thou that Saul and Jonathan his son be dead? And the young man that told him said, As I happened by chance upon mount Gilboa, behold, Saul leaned upon his spear; and, lo, the chariots and the horsemen followed hard after him. And when he looked behind him, he saw me, and called unto me. And I answered, Here am I. And he said unto me, Who art thou? And I answered him, I am an Amalekite. And he said unto me, Stand, I pray thee, beside me, and slay me, for anguish hath taken hold of me; because my life is yet whole in me. So I stood beside him, and slew him, because I was sure that he could not live after that he was fallen: and I took the crown that was upon his head, and the bracelet that was on his arm, and have brought them hither unto my lord. Then David took hold on his clothes, and rent them; and likewise all the men that were with him, and they mourned, and wept, and fasted until even, for Saul, and for Jonathan his son, and for the people of the LORD, and for the house of Israel; because they were fallen by the sword. And David said unto the young man that told him, Whence art thou? And he answered, I am the son of a stranger, an Amalekite. And David said unto him, How wast thou not afraid to put forth thine hand to destroy the LORD'S anointed? And David called one of the young men, and said, Go near, and fall upon him. And he smote him, that he died. And David said unto him, Thy blood be upon thy head; for thy mouth hath testified against thee, saying, I have slain the LORD's anointed.

And David lamented with this lamentation over Saul and over Jonathan his son.

David's Lament

>Thy glory, O Israel,
>Is slain upon thy high places!
>>*How are the mighty —*
>>*Fallen!*

Ye mountains of Gilboa, let there be no dew nor rain
    upon you,
Neither fields of offerings;
>For there the shield of the mighty was vilely cast away,
>The shield of Saul as of one not anointed with oil.

From the blood of the slain,
From the fat of the mighty,
>The bow of Jonathan turned not back,
>And the sword of Saul returned not empty.

Saul and Jonathan were lovely and pleasant in their lives,
And in their death they were not divided;
>They were swifter than eagles,
>They were stronger than lions.

David

Ye daughters of Israel,
Weep over Saul,
    Who clothed you in scarlet delicately,
    Who put ornaments of gold upon your apparel.

        How are the mighty —
        Fallen in the midst of the battle!
            O Jonathan,
              Slain upon thy high places,

I am distressed for thee, my brother Jonathan:
Very pleasant hast thou been unto me:
    Thy love to me was wonderful,
    Passing the love of women.

        How are the mighty —
           Fallen!
        And the weapons of war —
           Perished!

The Judges ⚔   Notes

Notes to the Judges

ii. *Old shoes and clouted: clouted* is patched.

iii. To understand thoroughly this celebrated story certain points must be borne in mind. (1) At different times different tribes of Israel take the lead; in the present case it is the northern tribes of Zebulun and Naphtali who are the heroes of the day. Other tribes are less eager, especially Reuben; its change of mind from *great resolves of heart* to *great searchings of heart* is laughed at in the Song of Deborah. Barak the commander-in-chief is of the tribe of Zebulun [*out of Zebulun they that handle the marshal's staff*]: the rallying place of the hosts is *Kedesh-naphtali* [great city, or capital, of Naphtali]. Deborah herself was of the tribe of Issachar. The different behaviour of the tribes is celebrated in the portion of the song called the Muster. (2) The Kenites were a people who had joined the Israelites during their journey through the wilderness, and had become by now a part of Israel, except that the Kenites continued their life in tents. Hence the importance of the statements that *Heber the Kenite had severed himself from the Kenites . . . and had pitched his tent as far as the oak . . . which is by Kedesh:* and again: *There was peace between Jabin . . . and the house of Heber:* and again: *They told Sisera that Barak . . . was gone up.* Putting these three passages together we can see that this Heber the Kenite was a spy, in the pay of the Canaanite king, and that he betrayed the movements of his allies the Israelites to their oppressor. But his wife Jael evidently hates this treachery, and plays the traitor on the other side, by slaying Sisera when he takes refuge in her tent. Nothing can excuse her treacherous murder: but the fact that it was done to atone for her false husband's treachery on the other side makes it easier to understand why the Song of Deborah mentions the deed with triumph, instead of condemning its wickedness. (3) On account of the 900 chariots of iron, which foot soldiers could not well fight against, the only hope for Israel was a surprise. Accordingly the plan was to muster silently, little by little on the hills, and seize a favourable moment for a rush upon Sisera's forces. But this was prevented by the treachery of Heber the Kenite, who reported to Sisera. The Canaanite army, with its chariots, thus filled the plain [called *Esdraelon:* hence this is the Battle of Esdraelon], which was just what was wanted for the free movements of chariots. All thus seemed hopeless for Israel. But a sudden thunderstorm came [*The stars in their courses fought against Sisera*], followed by fierce rain which swelled the waters of the river Kishon, until the whole plain was a marsh [hence the helpless *pransings of the strong* horses, trying to get out of the mud]. As a result Israel was able to destroy the whole army while they were caught in the marsh. — *Meroz* must have been some city on the line of retreat of the Canaanites, which failed to come promptly on this critical day. (4) The Song of Deborah, like other ancient poetry of the Hebrews, was accompanied with timbrel music and dancing: Deborah and the Women take one part, Barak and the Men take another, and sometimes they sing together. Probably the 'refrains' [printed in italics]

The Judges ~ Notes

were the parts where the timbrel music and dancing broke out most, though there would be some movement all through. To get the general effect, boys may take the men's part, girls the women's: while at the italic passages the recitation might be accompanied with clapping of the hands.

Page 125. *The LORD sold them into the hand of Jabin:* for the expression *sold* compare: *The wages of sin is death:* the LORD is poetically described as exchanging for the people's iniquity the price of slavery. — **Page 129.** *Tell of it ye that ride on white asses:* the ass was the regular animal for riding among the Israelites. The reference is to rulers. The Men call on all men to rejoice, whether rulers on asses or common people by the wayside; then the Women add how women, in their place of assembly, the places of drawing water, shall sing the same deliverance.

iv. The Midianites were a people leading a wandering life in the deserts, like the Arabian Bedouins we read of today. They had camels and gorgeous tents, and were formidable by their vast numbers. There are vast desert regions to the east of Palestine: hence Midianites and similar desert peoples are called *children of the east.* It is natural that the part of the holy land which suffered most in this war was Gilead, a region east of the river Jordan. *Manasseh, Asher, Zebulun, Naphtali,* are all tribes of Israel called upon to assist.

v. The Ammonites were a mountain people dwelling east of the Jordan. Israel had come into conflict with them while passing through the wilderness: and they continued through all their history border foes of the Israelites. — **Page 141.** *Bewail* *my virginity:* the great ambition of every Hebrew woman was to be the ancestress, perhaps even the mother, of the promised Messiah. Hence Jephthah's daughter bewails not her death, but that she must die before becoming a mother.

vi. *Ashkelon* is one of the main cities of the Philistines, all of which lie along the coast of the Mediterranean Sea. — *The cleft of the rock of Etam:* Samson had occupied some pass in the mountains, so narrow that he alone could hold it against a host. — *A Nazirite:* the total abstainers of that day: they were pledged to this from infancy, and in token of the pledge wore hair that was never cut.

vii. *A daughter of Belial:* of all the idolatries to which the Israelites yielded that of Belial was the most contemptible: hence *a man of Belial* became an expression for one contemptible in his wickedness. — 'Samuel' in the original means 'asked of God.' — *The word of the LORD was precious in those days: precious* is an old English word for scarce. In that period when the priests themselves were wicked the answers of God to inquirers became rare, and (like that to Samuel) secret: *There was no open vision.* — *God do so to thee, and more also:* this is a Hebrew saying, used in solemn charges. — *The ark of the covenant* was the sacred chest in which were deposited (among other things) the Tables written by the finger of God with the ten commandments: it was the most sacred emblem of the covenant between God and the Chosen People: the spot where it was kept was regarded as the very presence of God. Hence the terror of the Philistines when this ark was brought into the battle. — *Dagon:* the chief idol of the Philistines:

half man, half fish, the Philistines being a maritime people, whose cities lay along the coast of the Mediterranean.

viii. *The seer's house:* the Bible history has an explanation here: *He that is now called a Prophet was beforetime called a Seer.* — He *communed with Saul upon the housetop:* the flat roof of a Hebrew house was like the verandah of an American house, the regular place for resting and conversation. In the climate of that land they could often sleep there all night. — *A band of prophets:* from the time of Samuel we find regular schools of prophets, like the monasteries of the middle ages. The words of inspiration were accompanied with music and bodily motion or dancing.

x. Note how the three personages of this important story represent the three main weapons of ancient warfare: Saul is great with the spear, Jonathan is the hero of the bow and arrow, and David of the sling. These were the first forms of the modern cavalry, infantry, artillery. **Page 179.** *An evil spirit from God:* this is an expression of the same kind as that which says *God hardened Pharaoh's heart.* The consequences of sin, though they take the form of *an evil spirit,* are said to be sent by *God,* whose providence unites suffering with sinning. — **Page 180.** *The teraphim:* an idol image. — **Page 188.** *Saying, Go serve other gods:* in those days every different country had different religion: hence the driving David out of Israel was equivalent to bidding him serve other gods than the LORD.

BIBLE STORIES

THE KINGS AND THE PROPHETS

INTRODUCTION TO THE KINGS AND THE PROPHETS

In the fourth period of its history Israel was governed by visible kings. But a portion of the nation still stood for the idea of looking directly to the LORD for the guidance of his people. They were represented by a succession of 'prophets,' or 'interpreters of God,' who were inspired to make objections when the kings were leading the people astray. Thus the history of this period took the form of a government by kings and an opposition of prophets.

The Bible history now gives, in regular order, descriptions of the kings and accounts of the chief events of each reign. Such history cannot be well represented by extracts, but should be read as a whole. Its most important parts, however, are where the mere narrative of events is interrupted by the stories of the prophets, as they arose one after another to take part in Israel's affairs. It is chiefly these stories of the prophets which are represented in the present selection.

David was the founder of the Israelite monarchy. He was the first to gather the scattered settlements of his people into a united nation. He made the city of Jerusalem, which he captured from the Jebusites, his metropolis. Un-

Introduction   ⇥ Bible Stories

like other conquerors of history, he was a poet and musician, and laid the foundations of his country's literature. He also established a ritual of worship, and collected the materials for the Temple which his successor was to build. David was so much 'the man after God's own heart' that there was not much room in his reign for prophetic opposition. But one of our stories relates the great sin of David, and the prophet Nathan's rebuke. As one consequence of this sin David had continual trouble in his family, and a second story is devoted to the Rebellion of Absalom.

Solomon completed the Temple which his father had planned; this was the centre of the national religion, and one of the most wonderful buildings of antiquity. He also extended the commerce of Israel to distant parts of the world. But, while all this made Solomon's reign the most splendid portion of Israel's history, it also introduced luxury and other kinds of trouble. Solomon's greatest personal distinction is the fact that he appears as the founder of the Philosophy, or as it was called 'Wisdom,' of the Hebrews. One of the stories in this series is connected with the wisdom of Solomon.

Under Solomon's son Rehoboam the division took place, which is the subject of one of our stories. Henceforward there were two separate kingdoms. Only two of the twelve tribes followed Rehoboam, and these made up the kingdom of Judah; to this however belonged Jerusalem and the

Kings and Prophets ❧ Introduction

Temple. The ten tribes, under their leader Jeroboam, set up the northern Kingdom, usually called the kingdom of Israel, and built the great City of Samaria as a rival to Jerusalem.

The Bible history deals most fully with the northern kingdom of Israel, in which the chief struggle between kings and prophets took place. After a succession of many kings, and several revolutions, there came to the throne the supremely wicked family of Omri, of which the chief representative was King Ahab. He had for queen the infamous Jezebel, a princess of the great merchant city Zidon; in their reign the worship of the foreign god Baal was set up in Israel in antagonism with that of Jehovah. The crisis brought out Elijah, greatest of the prophets; and the Story of Elijah is here given at length. As Moses chose a successor in Joshua, so Elijah left Elisha to carry on his work: the wonder stories of this prophet are in part given below. The kingdom of Israel became more and more corrupt, until at last it fell before the Assyrians, the oriental people who were at that time overrunning large parts of the world. The ten tribes were carried away into captivity, and lost among the populations of the far East.

Meanwhile, the kingdom of Judah had its succession of rulers, its sins, and its revolutions; but taken as a whole showed much more fidelity to the worship of God than the sister kingdom. Two names stand out promi-

Introduction Bible Stories

nent from its list of kings. Under the pious Hezekiah Judah was threatened by Assyrian invasion, and Jerusalem was besieged by the armies of Sennacherib. Here appeared the great prophet Isaiah, and kept the king and people firm to their trust in the LORD. The famous story of the overthrow of Sennacherib is one of those here given. Josiah was no less pious than Hezekiah. In his reign was suddenly discovered the 'Book of the Law': what exactly this book was is not now known, but the discovery led to a religious revolution, which is commemorated in the final story of this series. At last the corrupted kingdom of Judah in its turn was overthrown by another Eastern people, the Chaldeans; and large part of the Jews carried captive to the Chaldean city of Babylon.

STORIES FROM THE KINGS AND THE PROPHETS

   i. David and the Prophet Nathan
  ii. The Revolt of Absalom
 iii. The Wisdom of Solomon
 iv. Story of the Divided Kingdom
  v. Stories of the Prophet Elijah
      Elijah and the Prophets of Baal
      Elijah in the Desert
      The Story of Naboth's Vineyard
      Ascent of Elijah to Heaven
 vi. Stories of the Prophet Elisha
      The Shunammite's Son
      Naaman and Gehazi
 vii. The Assyrian Army and the Prophet Isaiah
viii. Josiah and the Finding of the Law

i

David and the Prophet Nathan

And it came to pass, that David walked upon the roof of the king's house: and from the roof he saw a woman: and the woman was very beautiful to look upon. And David sent and inquired after the woman. And one said, Is not this Bath-sheba, the wife of Uriah the Hittite? And David sent messengers, and took her.

And David wrote a letter to Joab, saying, Set ye Uriah in the forefront of the hottest battle, and retire ye from him, that he may be smitten, and die. And it came to pass, when Joab kept watch upon the city, that he assigned Uriah unto the place where he knew that valiant men were. And the men of the city went out, and fought with Joab: and there fell some of the people, even of the servants of David; and Uriah the Hittite died also. And when the wife of Uriah heard that Uriah her husband was dead, she made lamentation for her husband. And when the mourning was past, David sent and took her home to his house, and she became his wife, and bare him a son. But the thing that David had done displeased the LORD.

And the LORD sent Nathan unto David. And he came

unto him, and said unto him, There were two men in one city; the one rich, and the other poor. The rich man had exceeding many flocks and herds: but the poor man had nothing, save one little ewe lamb, which he had bought and nourished up: and it grew up together with him, and with his children; it did eat of his own morsel, and drank of his own cup, and lay in his bosom, and was unto him as a daughter. And there came a traveller unto the rich man, and he spared to take of his own flock and of his own herd, to dress for the wayfaring man that was come unto him, but took the poor man's lamb, and dressed it for the man that was come to him. And David's anger was greatly kindled against the man; and he said to Nathan, As the LORD liveth, the man that hath done this is worthy to die: and he shall restore the lamb fourfold, because he did this thing, and because he had no pity. And Nathan said to David, Thou art the man. Thus saith the LORD, the God of Israel, I anointed thee king over Israel, and I delivered thee out of the hand of Saul; and I gave thee thy master's house, and gave thee the house of Israel and of Judah; and if that had been too little, I would have added unto thee such and such things. Wherefore hast thou despised the word of the LORD, to do that which is evil in his sight? thou hast smitten Uriah the Hittite with the sword, and hast taken his wife to be thy wife, and hast slain him with the sword of the children of Ammon. Now therefore, the sword shall never depart from thine house. And David said unto Nathan, I have sinned against the LORD. And Nathan said unto David, The LORD also hath put away thy sin; thou shalt not die. Howbeit, because by this deed thou hast given great occasion to the enemies of the LORD to blaspheme, the child also that is born unto thee shall surely die. And Nathan departed unto his house.

ii

The Revolt of Absalom

Now in all Israel there was none to be so much praised as Absalom for his beauty: from the sole of his foot even to the crown of his head there was no blemish in him. And when he polled his head, (now it was at every year's end that he polled it: because the hair was heavy on him, therefore he polled it:) he weighed the hair of his head at two hundred shekels, after the king's weight.

And it came to pass, that Absalom prepared him a chariot and horses, and fifty men to run before him. And Absalom rose up early, and stood beside the way of the gate: and it was so, that when any man had a suit which should come to the king for judgement, then Absalom called unto him, and said, Of what city art thou? And he said, Thy servant is of one of the tribes of Israel. And

Absalom said unto him, See, thy matters are good and right; but there is no man deputed of the king to hear thee. Absalom said moreover, Oh that I were made judge in the land, that every man which hath any suit or cause might come unto me, and I would do him justice! And it was so, that when any man came nigh to do him obeisance, he put forth his hand, and took hold of him, and kissed him. And on this manner did Absalom to all Israel that came to the king for judgement: so Absalom stole the hearts of the men of Israel.

And there came a messenger to David, saying, The hearts of the men of Israel are after Absalom. And David said unto all his servants that were with him at Jerusalem, Arise, and let us flee; for else none of us shall escape from Absalom: make speed to depart, lest he overtake us quickly, and bring down evil upon us, and smite the city with the edge of the sword. And the king's servants said unto the king, Behold, thy servants are ready to do whatsoever my lord the king shall choose. And the king went forth, and all his household after him.

And David went up by the ascent of the mount of Olives, and wept as he went up; and he had his head covered, and went barefoot: and all the people that were with him covered every man his head, and they went up, weeping as they went up.

And when king David came to Bahurim, behold, there came out thence a man of the family of the house of Saul, whose name was Shimei: he came out, and cursed still as he came. And he cast stones at David, and at all the servants of king David: and all the people and all the mighty men were on his right hand and on his left. And thus said Shimei when he cursed, Begone, begone, thou man of blood, and man of Belial: the LORD hath returned upon thee all the blood of the house of Saul, in whose stead thou hast reigned; and the LORD hath delivered the kingdom into the hand of Absalom thy son: and, behold, thou art taken in thine own mischief, because thou art a man of blood. Then said Abishai the son of Zeruiah unto the king, Why should this dead dog curse my lord the king? let me go over, I pray thee, and take off his head. And the king said, Because he curseth, and because the LORD hath said unto him, Curse David; who then shall say, Wherefore hast thou done so? And David said to Abishai, and to all his servants, Behold, my son seeketh my life: how much more may this Benjamite now do it? let him alone, and let him curse; for the LORD hath bidden him. It may be that the LORD will look on the wrong done unto me, and that the LORD will requite me good for his cursing of me this day. So David and his men went by the way: and Shimei went along on the hill side over against him, and cursed as he went, and threw stones at him, and cast dust.

Then David came to Mahanaim. And Absalom passed over Jordan, he and all the men of Israel with him. And

Israel and Absalom pitched in the land of Gilead. And David numbered the people that were with him, and set captains of thousands and captains of hundreds over them. And the king said unto the people, I will surely go forth with you myself also. But the people said, Thou shalt not go forth: for if we flee away, they will not care for us; neither if half of us die, will they care for us: but thou art worth ten thousand of us: therefore now it is better that thou be ready to succour us out of the city. And the king said unto them, What seemeth you best I will do. And the king stood by the gate side, and all the people went out by hundreds and by thousands. And the king commanded, saying, Deal gently for my sake with the young man, even with Absalom. And all the people heard when the king gave all the captains charge concerning Absalom. So the people went out into the field against Israel: and the battle was in the forest of Ephraim. And the people of Israel were smitten there before the servants of David, and there was a great slaughter there that day of twenty thousand men. For the battle was there spread over the face of all the country: and the forest devoured more people that day than the sword devoured. And Absalom chanced to meet the servants of David. And Absalom rode upon his mule, and the mule went under the thick boughs of a great oak, and his head caught hold of the oak, and he was taken up between the heaven and the earth; and the mule that was under him went on.

And a certain man saw it, and told Joab, and said, Behold, I saw Absalom hanging in an oak. And Joab said unto the man that told him, And, behold, thou sawest it, and why didst thou not smite him there to the ground? and I would have given thee ten pieces of silver, and a girdle. And the man said unto Joab, Though I should receive a thousand pieces of silver in mine hand, yet would I not put forth mine hand against the king's son: for in our hearing the king charged, saying, Beware that none touch the young man Absalom. Otherwise if I had dealt falsely against his life, (and there is no matter hid from the king,) then thou thyself wouldest have stood aloof. Then said Joab, I may not tarry thus with thee. And he took three darts in his hand, and thrust them through the heart of Absalom, while he was yet alive in the midst of the oak. And ten young men that bare Joab's armour compassed about and smote Absalom, and slew him. And Joab blew the trumpet, and the people returned from pursuing after Israel: for Joab held back the people. And they took Absalom and cast him into the great pit in the forest, and raised over him a very great heap of stones: and all Israel fled every one to his tent.

Then said Ahimaaz the son of Zadok, Let me now run, and bear the king tidings, how that the LORD hath avenged him of his enemies. And Joab said unto him, Thou shalt not be the bearer of tidings this day, but thou shalt bear tidings another day: but this day thou shalt bear no tidings, because the king's son is dead. Then said Joab to the Cushite, Go tell the king what thou hast seen. And the Cushite bowed himself unto Joab, and ran. Then said Ahimaaz the son of Zadok yet again to Joab, But come what may, let me, I pray thee, also run after the Cushite. And Joab said, Wherefore wilt thou run, my son, seeing that thou wilt have no reward for the tidings? But come what may, said he, I will run. And he said unto him, Run. Then Ahimaaz ran by the way of the Plain, and overran the Cushite.

Now David sat between the two gates: and the watchman went up to the roof of the gate unto the wall, and lifted up his eyes, and looked, and, behold, a man running alone. And the watchman cried, and told the king. And the king said, If he be alone, there is tidings in his mouth. And he came apace, and drew near. And the watchman saw another man running: and the watchman called unto the porter, and said, Behold, another man running alone. And the king said, He also bringeth tidings. And the watchman said, Me thinketh the running of the foremost is like the running of Ahimaaz the son of Zadok. And the king said, He is a good man, and cometh with good tidings. And Ahimaaz called, and said unto the king, All is well. And he bowed himself before the king with his face to the earth, and said, Blessed be the LORD thy God, which hath delivered up the men that lifted up their hand against my lord the king. And the king said, Is it well with the young man Absalom? And Ahimaaz answered, When Joab sent the king's servant, even me thy servant, I saw a great tumult, but I knew not what it was. And the king said, Turn aside, and stand here. And he turned aside, and stood still. And, behold, the Cushite came; and the Cushite said, Tidings for my lord the king: for the Lord hath avenged thee this day of all them that rose up against thee. And the king said unto the Cushite, Is it well with the young man Absalom? And the Cushite answered, The enemies of my lord the king, and all that rise up against thee to do thee hurt, be as that young man is. And the king was much moved, and went up to the chamber over the gate and wept: and as he went, thus he said, O my son Absalom, my son, my son Absalom! would God I had died for thee, O Absalom, my son, my son!

iii

The Wisdom of Solomon

And the king went to Gibeon to sacrifice there; for that was the great high place: a thousand burnt offerings did Solomon offer upon that altar. In Gibeon the Lord appeared to Solomon in a dream by night: and God said, Ask what I shall give thee. And Solomon said, Thou hast shewed unto thy servant David my father great kindness, according as he walked before thee in truth, and in righteousness, and in uprightness of heart with thee; and thou hast kept for him this great kindness, that thou hast given him a son to sit on his throne, as it is this day. And now, O LORD my God, thou hast made thy servant king instead of David my father: and I am but a little child; I know not how to go out or come in. And thy servant is in the midst of thy people which thou hast chosen, a great people, that cannot be numbered nor counted for multitude. Give thy servant therefore an understanding heart to judge thy people, that I may discern between good and evil; for who is able to judge this thy great people? And the speech pleased the Lord, that Solomon had asked this thing. And God said unto him, Because thou hast asked this thing, and hast not asked for thyself long life; neither hast asked riches for thyself, nor hast asked the life of thine enemies; but hast asked for thyself understanding to discern judgement; behold, I have done according to thy word: lo, I have given thee a wise and an understanding heart; so that there hath been none like thee before thee, neither after thee shall any arise like unto thee. And I have also given thee that which thou hast not asked, both riches and honour, so that there shall not be any among the kings like unto thee, all thy days. And if thou wilt walk in my ways, to keep my statutes and my commandments, as thy father David did walk, then I will lengthen thy days. And Solomon awoke, and behold, it was a dream: and he came to Jerusalem, and stood before the ark of the covenant of the LORD, and offered up burnt offerings, and offered peace offerings, and made a feast to all his servants.

Then came there two women unto the king, and stood before him. And the one woman said, Oh my lord, I and this woman dwell in one house; and we were together; there was no stranger with us in the house, save we two in the house. And this woman's child died in the night; because she overlaid it. And she arose at midnight, and took my son from beside me, while thine handmaid slept, and laid it in her bosom, and laid her dead child in my bosom. And when I rose in the morning to give my child suck, behold, it was dead: but when I had considered it in the morning, behold, it was not my son, which I did bear. And the other woman said, Nay; but the living is my son, and the dead is thy son. And this said No; but the dead is thy son, and the living is my son. Thus they spake before the king. Then said the king, The one saith, This is my son that liveth, and thy son is the dead: and the other saith, Nay; but thy son is the dead, and my son is the living. And the king said, Fetch me a sword. And they brought a sword before the king. And the king said, Divide the living child in two, and give half to the one, and half to the other. Then spake the woman whose the living child was unto the king, Oh my lord, give her the living child, and in no wise slay it. But the other said, It shall be neither mine nor thine; divide it. Then the king answered and said, Give her the living child, and in no wise slay it: she is the mother thereof. And all Israel heard of the judgement which the king had judged; and they feared the king: for they saw that the wisdom of God was in him, to do judgement.

And when the queen of Sheba heard of the fame of Solomon concerning the name of the LORD, she came to prove him with hard questions. And she came to Jerusalem with a very great train, with camels that bare spices, and very much gold, and precious stones: and when she was come to Solomon, she communed with him of all that was in her heart. And Solomon told her all her questions: there was not anything hid from the king which he told her not. And when the queen of Sheba had seen all the wisdom of Solomon, and the house that he had built, and the meat of his table, and the sitting of his servants, and the attendance of his ministers, and their apparel, and his cupbearers, and his ascent by which he went up unto the house of the LORD; there was no more spirit in her. And she said to the king, It was a true report that I heard in mine own land of thine acts, and of thy wisdom. Howbeit I believed not the words, until I came, and mine eyes had seen it: and, behold, the half was not told me: thy wisdom and prosperity exceedeth the fame which I heard.

Happy are thy men, happy are these thy servants, which stand continually before thee, and that hear thy wisdom. Blessed be the LORD thy God, which delighted in thee, to set thee on the throne of Israel: because the LORD loved Israel for ever, therefore made he thee king, to do judgement and justice.

iv

Story of the Divided Kingdom

And Rehoboam went to Shechem: for all Israel were come to Shechem to make him king. And it came to pass, when Jeroboam the son of Nebat heard of it, that Jeroboam and all the congregation of Israel came, and spake unto Rehoboam, saying, Thy father made our yoke grievous: now therefore make thou the grievous service of thy father, and his heavy yoke which he put upon us, lighter, and we will serve thee. And he said unto them, Depart yet for three days, then come again to me. And the people departed.

And king Rehoboam took counsel with the old men, that had stood before Solomon his father while he yet lived, saying, What counsel give ye me to return answer to this people? And they spake unto him, saying, If thou wilt be a servant unto this people this day, and wilt serve them, and answer them, and speak good words to them, then they will be thy servants for ever. But he forsook the counsel of the old men which they had given him, and took counsel with the young men that were grown up with him, that stood before him. And he said unto them, What counsel give ye that we may return answer to this people, who have spoken to me, saying, Make the yoke that thy father did put upon us lighter? And the young men that were grown up with him spake unto him, saying, Thus shalt thou say unto this people that spake unto thee, saying, Thy father made our yoke heavy, but make thou it lighter unto us; thus shalt thou speak unto them, My little finger is thicker than my father's loins. And now whereas my father did lade you with a heavy yoke, I will add to your yoke: my father chastised you with whips, but I will chastise you with scorpions.

So Jeroboam and all the people came to Rehoboam the third day, as the king bade, saying, Come to me again the third day. And the king answered the people roughly, and forsook the counsel of the old men which they had given him; and spake to them after the counsel of the young men, saying, My father made your yoke heavy, but I will add to your yoke: my father chastised you with whips, but I will chastise you with scorpions. So the king hearkened not unto the people; and when all Israel saw that the king hearkened not unto them, the people answered the king, saying, What portion have we in David?

neither have we inheritance in the son of Jesse: to your tents, O Israel: now see to thine own house, David. So Israel departed unto their tents. But as for the children of Israel which dwelt in the cities of Judah, Rehoboam reigned over them.

V

Stories of the Prophet Elijah

Elijah and the Prophets of Baal

And Ahab the son of Omri reigned over Israel in Samaria twenty and two years. And Ahab the son of Omri did that which was evil in the sight of the LORD above all that were before him. And he took to wife Jezebel the daughter of Ethbaal king of the Zidonians, and went and served Baal, and worshipped him. And he reared up an altar for Baal in the house of Baal, which he had built in Samaria.

And Elijah the Tishbite said unto Ahab, As the LORD, the God of Israel, liveth, before whom I stand, there shall not be dew nor rain these years, but according to my word. And the word of the LORD came unto him, saying, Get thee hence, and turn thee eastward, and hide thyself by the brook Cherith, that is before Jordan. And it shall be, that thou shalt drink of the brook; and I have commanded the ravens to feed thee there. So he went and did according unto the word of the LORD: for he went and dwelt by the brook Cherith, that is before Jordan. And the ravens brought him bread and flesh in the morning, and bread and flesh in the evening; and he drank of the brook.

And it came to pass after many days, that the word of the LORD came to Elijah, in the third year, saying, Go, shew thyself unto Ahab; and I will send rain upon the earth. And Elijah went to shew himself unto Ahab. And the famine was sore in Samaria. And Ahab called Obadiah, which was over the household. (Now Obadiah feared the LORD greatly: for it was so, when Jezebel cut off the prophets of the LORD, that Obadiah took an hundred prophets, and hid them by fifty in a cave, and fed them with bread and water.) And Ahab said unto Obadiah, Go through the land, unto all the fountains of water, and unto all the brooks: peradventure we may find grass and save the horses and mules alive, that we lose not all the beasts. So they divided the land between them to pass throughout it: Ahab went one way by himself, and Obadiah went another way by himself. And as Obadiah was in the way, behold, Elijah met him: and he knew him, and fell on his face, and said, Is it thou, my lord Elijah? And he answered him, It is I: go, tell thy lord, Behold, Elijah is here. And he said, Wherein have I sinned, that thou wouldest deliver thy servant into the hand of Ahab, to slay me? As the LORD thy God liveth, there is no nation or kingdom, whither my lord hath not sent to seek thee: and when they said, He is not here, he took an oath of the kingdom and nation, that they found thee not. And now thou sayest, Go, tell thy lord, Behold, Elijah is here. And it shall come to pass, as soon as I am gone from thee, that the spirit of the LORD shall carry thee whither I know not; and so when I come and tell Ahab, and he cannot find thee, he shall slay me: but I thy servant fear the LORD from my youth. Was it not told my lord what I did when Jezebel slew the prophets of the LORD, how I hid an hundred men of the LORD'S prophets by fifty in a cave, and fed them with bread and water? And now thou sayest, Go, tell thy lord, Behold, Elijah is here: and he shall slay me. And Elijah said, As the LORD of hosts liveth, before whom I stand, I will surely shew myself unto him today. So Obadiah went to meet Ahab, and told him: and Ahab went to meet Elijah. And it came to pass, when Ahab saw Elijah, that Ahab said unto him, Is it thou, thou troubler of Israel? And he answered, I have not troubled Israel; but thou, and thy father's house, in that ye have forsaken the commandments of the LORD, and thou hast followed the Baalim. Now therefore send, and gather to me all Israel unto mount Carmel, and the prophets of Baal four hundred and fifty, and the prophets of the Asherah four hundred, which eat at Jezebel's table.

So Ahab sent unto all the children of Israel, and gathered the prophets together unto mount Carmel. And Elijah came near unto all the people, and said, How long halt ye between two opinions? if the LORD be God, follow him: but if Baal, then follow him. And the people answered him not a word. Then said Elijah unto the people, I, even I only, am left a prophet of the LORD; but Baal's prophets are four hundred and fifty men. Let them therefore give us two bullocks; and let them choose one bullock for themselves, and cut it in pieces, and lay it on the wood, and put no fire under: and I will dress the other bullock, and lay it on the wood, and put no fire under. And call ye on the name of your god, and I will call on the name of the LORD: and the God that answereth by fire, let him be God. And all the people answered and said, It is well spoken. And Elijah said unto the prophets of Baal, Choose you one bullock for yourselves, and dress it first; for ye are many; and call on the name of your god, but put no fire under. And they took the bullock which was given them, and they dressed it, and called on the name of Baal from morning even until noon, saying, O Baal, hear us. But there was no voice, nor any that answered. And they leaped about the altar which was made. And it came to pass at noon, that Elijah mocked them, and said, Cry aloud: for he is a god; either he is musing, or he is gone aside, or he is in a journey, or peradventure he sleepeth, and must be awaked. And they cried aloud, and cut themselves after their manner with knives and lances, till the blood gushed out upon them.

Kings and Prophets   Elijah

And it was so, when midday was past, that they prophesied until the time of the offering of the evening oblation; but there was neither voice, nor any to answer, nor any that regarded. And Elijah said unto all the people, Come near unto me; and all the people came near unto him. And he repaired the altar of the LORD that was thrown down. And Elijah took twelve stones, according to the number of the tribes of the sons of Jacob, unto whom the word of the LORD came, saying, Israel shall be thy name. And with the stones he built an altar in the name of the LORD; and he made a trench about the altar, as great as would contain two measures of seed. And he put the wood in order, and cut the bullock in pieces, and laid it on the wood. And he said, Fill four barrels with water, and pour it on the burnt offering, and on the wood. And he said, Do it the second time; and they did it the second time. And he said, Do it the third time; and they did it the third time. And the water ran round about the altar; and he filled the trench also with water. And it came to pass at the time of the offering of the evening oblation, that Elijah the prophet came near, and said, O LORD, the God of Abraham, of Isaac, and of Israel, let it be known this day that thou art God in Israel, and that I am thy servant, and that I have done all these things at thy word. Hear me, O LORD, hear me, that this people may know that thou, LORD, art God, and that thou hast turned their heart back again. Then the fire of the LORD fell, and consumed

Elijah — **Bible Stories**

the burnt offering, and the wood, and the stones, and the dust, and licked up the water that was in the trench. And when all the people saw it, they fell on their faces: and they said, The LORD, he is God; the LORD, he is God. And Elijah said unto them, Take the prophets of Baal; let not one of them escape. And they took them: and Elijah brought them down to the brook Kishon, and slew them there. And Elijah said unto Ahab, Get thee up, eat and drink; for there is the sound of abundance of rain. So Ahab went up to eat and to drink. And Elijah went up to the top of Carmel; and he bowed himself down upon the earth, and put his face between his knees. And he said to his servant, Go up now, look toward the sea. And he went up, and looked, and said, There is nothing. And he said, Go again seven times. And it came to pass at the seventh time, that he said, Behold, there ariseth a cloud out of the sea, as small as a man's hand. And he said, Go up, say unto Ahab, Make ready thy chariot, and get thee down, that the rain stop thee not. And it came to pass in a little while, that the heaven grew black with clouds and wind, and there was a great rain. And Ahab rode and went to Jezreel. And the hand of the LORD was on Elijah; and he girded up his loins, and ran before Ahab to the entrance of Jezreel.

Kings and Prophets   Elijah

Elijah in the Desert

And Ahab told Jezebel all that Elijah had done, and withal how he had slain all the prophets with the sword. Then Jezebel sent a messenger unto Elijah, saying, So let the gods do to me, and more also, if I make not thy life as the life of one of them by tomorrow about this time. And when he saw that, he arose, and went for his life, and came to Beer-sheba, which belongeth to Judah, and left his servant there. But he himself went a day's journey into the wilderness, and came and sat down under a juniper tree: and he requested for himself that he might die; and said, It is enough; now, O Lord, take away my life; for I am not better than my fathers. And he lay down and slept under a juniper tree; and, behold, an angel touched him, and said unto him, Arise and eat. And he looked, and, behold, there was at his head a cake baken on the coals, and a cruse of water. And he did eat and drink, and laid him down again. And the angel of the Lord came again the second time, and touched him, and said, Arise and eat; because the journey is too great for thee. And he arose, and did eat and drink, and went in the strength of that meat forty days and forty nights unto Horeb the mount of God. And he came thither unto a cave, and lodged there; and, behold, the word of the Lord came to him, and he said unto him, What doest thou here, Elijah? And he said, I have been very jealous for the LORD, the God of hosts; for the children of Israel have forsaken thy covenant, thrown down thine altars, and slain thy prophets with the sword: and I, even I only, am left; and they seek my life, to take it away. And he said, Go forth, and stand upon the mount before the LORD. And, behold, the LORD passed by, and a great and strong wind rent the mountains, and brake in pieces the rocks before the LORD; but the LORD was not in the wind: and after the wind an earthquake; but the LORD was not in the earthquake: and after the earthquake a fire; but the LORD was not in the fire: and after the fire a still small voice. And it was so, when Elijah heard it, that he wrapped his face in his mantle, and went out, and stood in the entering in of the cave. And, behold, there came a voice unto him, and said, What doest thou here, Elijah? And he said, I have been very jealous for the LORD, the God of hosts; for the children of Israel have forsaken thy covenant, thrown down thine altars, and slain thy prophets with the sword; and I, even I only, am left; and they seek my life, to take it away. And the LORD said unto him, Go, return on thy way to the wilderness of Damascus: and when thou comest, thou shalt anoint Hazael to be king over Syria: and Jehu the son of Nimshi shalt thou anoint to be king over Israel: and Elisha the son of Shaphat shalt thou anoint to be prophet in thy room. And it shall come to pass, that him that escapeth from the sword of Hazael shall Jehu slay:

and him that escapeth from the sword of Jehu shall Elisha slay. Yet will I leave me seven thousand in Israel, all the knees which have not bowed unto Baal, and every mouth which hath not kissed him. So he departed thence, and found Elisha the son of Shaphat, who was ploughing, with twelve yoke of oxen before him, and he with the twelfth: and Elijah passed over unto him, and cast his mantle upon him. And he left the oxen, and ran after Elijah, and said, Let me, I pray thee, kiss my father and my mother, and then I will follow thee. And he said unto him, Go back again; for what have I done to thee? And he returned from following him, and took the yoke of oxen, and slew them, and boiled their flesh with the instruments of the oxen, and gave unto the people, and they did eat. Then he arose, and went after Elijah, and ministered unto him.

The Story of Naboth's Vineyard

And it came to pass after these things, that Naboth the Jezreelite had a vineyard, which was in Jezreel, hard by the palace of Ahab king of Samaria. And Ahab spake unto Naboth, saying, Give me thy vineyard, that I may have it for a garden of herbs, because it is near unto my house; and I will give thee for it a better vineyard than it: or, if it seem good to thee, I will give thee the worth of it in money. And Naboth said to Ahab, The LORD forbid it me, that I should give the inheritance of my fathers unto thee. And Ahab came into his house heavy and displeased because of the word which Naboth the Jezreelite had spoken to him: for he had said, I will not give thee the inheritance of my fathers. And he laid him down upon his bed, and turned away his face, and would eat no bread. But Jezebel his wife came to him, and said unto him, Why is thy spirit so sad, that thou eatest no bread? And he said unto her, Because I spake unto Naboth the Jezreelite, and said unto him, Give me thy vineyard for money; or else, if it please thee, I will give thee another vineyard for it: and he answered, I will not give thee my vineyard. And Jezebel his wife said unto him, Dost thou now govern the kingdom of Israel? arise, and eat bread, and let thine heart be merry: I will give thee the vineyard of Naboth the Jezreelite. So she wrote letters in Ahab's name, and sealed them with his seal, and sent the letters unto the elders and to the nobles that were in his city, and that dwelt with Naboth. And she wrote in the letters, saying, Proclaim a fast, and set Naboth on high among the people: and set two men, sons of Belial, before him, and let them bear witness against him, saying, Thou didst curse God and the king. And then carry him out, and stone him, that he die. And the men of his city, even the elders and the nobles who dwelt in his city, did as Jezebel had sent unto them, according as it was written in the letters which she had sent unto them. They proclaimed a fast, and set Naboth on high among the people. And the two men, sons of Belial, came in and sat before him: and the men of Belial bare witness against him, even against Naboth, in the presence of the people, saying, Naboth did curse God and the king. Then they carried him forth out of the city, and stoned him with stones, that he died. Then they sent to Jezebel, saying, Naboth is stoned, and is dead. And it came to pass, when Jezebel heard that Naboth was stoned, and was dead, that Jezebel said to Ahab, Arise, take possession of the vineyard of Naboth the Jezreelite, which he refused to give thee for money: for Naboth is not alive, but dead. And it came to pass, when Ahab heard that Naboth was dead, that Ahab rose up to go down to the vineyard of Naboth the Jezreelite, to take possession of it.

And the word of the LORD came to Elijah the Tishbite, saying, Arise, go down to meet Ahab king of Israel, which dwelleth in Samaria: behold, he is in the vineyard of Naboth, whither he is gone down to take possession of it. And thou shalt speak unto him, saying, Thus saith the LORD, Hast thou killed, and also taken possession? and thou shalt speak unto him, saying, Thus saith the LORD, In the place where dogs licked the blood of Naboth shall dogs lick thy blood, even thine. And Ahab said to Elijah, Hast thou found me, O mine enemy? And he answered, I have found thee: because thou hast sold thyself to do that which is evil in the sight of the LORD. Behold, I will bring evil upon thee, and will utterly sweep thee away, and will cut off from Ahab every man child, and him that is shut up and him that is left at large in Israel. And of Jezebel also spake the LORD, saying, The dogs shall eat Jezebel by the rampart of Jezreel. And it came to pass, when Ahab heard those words, that he rent his clothes, and put sackcloth upon his flesh, and fasted, and lay in sackcloth, and went softly. And the word of the LORD came to Elijah the Tishbite, saying, Seest thou how Ahab humbleth himself before me? because he humbleth himself before me I will not bring the evil in his days: but in his son's days will I bring the evil upon his house.

Ascent of Elijah to Heaven

And it came to pass when the LORD would take up Elijah by a whirlwind into heaven, that Elijah went with Elisha from Gilgal. And Elijah said unto Elisha, Tarry here, I pray thee; for the LORD hath sent me as far as Beth-el. And Elisha said, As the LORD liveth, and as thy soul liveth, I will not leave thee. So they went down to Beth-el. And the sons of the prophets that were at Beth-el came forth to Elisha, and said unto him, Knowest thou that the LORD will take away thy master from thy head today? And he said, Yea, I know it; hold ye your peace. And Elijah said unto him, Elisha, tarry here, I pray thee; for the LORD hath sent me to Jericho. And he said, As the LORD liveth, and as thy soul liveth, I will not leave thee. So they came to Jericho. And the sons of the prophets that were at Jericho came near to Elisha, and said unto him, Knowest thou that the LORD will take away thy master from thy head today? And he answered, Yea, I know it; hold ye your peace. And Elijah said unto him, Tarry here, I pray thee; for the LORD hath sent me to Jordan. And he said, As the LORD liveth, and as thy soul liveth, I will not leave thee. And they two went on. And fifty men of the sons of the prophets went, and stood over against them afar off: and they two stood by Jordan. And Elijah took his mantle, and wrapped it together, and smote the waters, and they were divided hither and thither, so that they two went over on dry ground. And it came to pass, when they were gone over, that Elijah said unto Elisha, Ask what I shall do for thee, before I be taken from thee. And Elisha said, I pray thee, let a double portion of thy spirit be upon me. And he said, Thou hast asked a hard thing: nevertheless, if thou see me when I am taken from thee, it shall be so unto thee; but if not, it shall not be so. And it came to pass, as they still went on, and talked, that, behold, there appeared a chariot of fire, and horses of fire, which parted them both asunder; and Elijah went up by a whirlwind into heaven. And Elisha saw it, and he cried, My father, my father, the chariots of Israel and the horsemen thereof! And he saw him no more: and he took hold of his own clothes, and rent them in two pieces. He took up also the mantle of Elijah that fell from him, and went back, and stood by the bank of Jordan. And he took the mantle of Elijah that fell from him, and smote the waters, and said, Where is the LORD, the God of Elijah? and when he also had smitten the waters, they were divided hither and thither: and Elisha went over. And when the sons of the prophets which were at Jericho over against him saw him, they said, The spirit of Elijah doth rest on Elisha.

vi

Stories of the Prophet Elisha

The Shunammite's Son

And it fell on a day, that Elisha passed to Shunem, where was a great woman; and she constrained him to eat bread. And so it was, that as oft as he passed by, he turned in thither to eat bread. And she said unto her husband, Behold, now, I perceive that this is a holy man of God, which passeth by us continually. Let us make, I pray thee, a little chamber on the wall; and let us set for him there a bed, and a table, and a stool, and a candlestick: and it shall be, when he cometh to us, that he shall turn in thither. And it fell on a day, that he came thither, and he turned into the chamber, and lay there. And he said to Gehazi his servant, Call this Shunammite. And when he had called her, she stood before him. And he said unto him, Say now unto her, Behold, thou hast been careful for us with all this care; what is to be done for thee? wouldest thou be spoken for to the king, or to the captain of the host? And she answered, I dwell among mine own people. And he said, What then is to be done for her? And Gehazi answered, Verily she hath no son. And he said, Call her. And when he had called her, she stood in the door. And he said, At this season, when the time cometh round, thou shalt embrace a son. And she said, Nay, my lord, thou man of God, do not lie unto thine handmaid. And the woman bare a son at that season, when the time came around, as Elisha had said unto her.

And when the child was grown, it fell on a day, that he went out to his father to the reapers. And he said unto his father, My head, my head! And he said to his servant, Carry him to his mother. And when he had taken him, and brought him to his mother, he sat on her knees till noon, and then died. And she went up, and laid him on the bed of the man of God, and shut the door upon him, and went out. And she called unto her husband, and said, Send me, I pray thee, one of the servants; and one of the asses, that I may run to the man of God and come again. And he said, Wherefore wilt thou go to him today? it is neither new moon nor sabbath. And she said, It shall be well. Then she saddled an ass, and said to her servant, Drive, and go forward; slacken me not the riding, except I bid thee. So she went and came unto the man of God to mount Carmel. And it came to pass, when the man of God saw her afar off, that he said to Gehazi his servant, Behold, yonder is the Shunammite: run, I pray thee, now to meet her, and say unto her, Is it well with thee? is it well with thy husband? is it well with the child? And she answered, It is well. And when she came to the man of God to the hill, she caught hold of his feet. And Gehazi came near to thrust her away; but the man of God said, Let her alone, for her soul is vexed within her; and the LORD hath hid it from me, and hath not told me. Then she said, Did I desire a son of my lord? did I not say, Do not deceive me? Then he said to Gehazi, Gird up thy loins, and take my staff in thine hand, and go thy way: if thou meet any man, salute him not; and if any salute thee, answer him not again: and lay my staff upon the face of the child. And the mother of the child said, As the LORD liveth, and as thy soul liveth, I will not leave thee. And he arose, and followed her. And Gehazi passed on before them, and laid the staff upon the face of the child; but there was neither voice, nor hearing. Wherefore he returned to meet him, and told him saying, The child is not awaked. And when Elisha was come into the house, behold, the child was dead, and laid upon his bed. He went in therefore, and shut the door upon them twain, and prayed unto the LORD. And he went up, and lay upon the child, and put his mouth upon his mouth, and his eyes upon his eyes, and his hands upon his hands: and he stretched himself upon him; and the flesh of the child waxed warm. Then he returned, and walked in the house once to and fro; and went up, and stretched himself upon him: and the child sneezed seven times, and the child opened his eyes. And he called Gehazi, and said, Call this Shunammite. So he called her. And when she was come in unto him, he said, Take up thy son. Then she went in, and fell at his feet, and bowed herself to the ground; and she took up her son, and went out.

Naaman and Gehazi

Now Naaman, captain of the host of the king of Syria, was a great man with his master, and honourable, because by him the LORD had given victory unto Syria: he was also a mighty man of valour, but he was a leper. And the Syrians had gone out in bands, and had brought away captive out of the land of Israel a little maid; and she waited on Naaman's wife. And she said unto her mistress, Would God my lord were with the prophet that is in Samaria! then would he recover him of his leprosy. And one went in, and told his lord, saying, Thus and thus said the maid that is of the land of Israel. And the king of Syria said, Go to, go, and I will send a letter unto the king of Israel. And he departed, and took with him ten talents of silver, and six thousand pieces of gold, and ten changes of raiment. And he brought the letter to the king of Israel, saying, And now when this letter is come unto thee, behold, I have sent Naaman my servant to thee, that thou mayest recover him of his leprosy. And it came to pass, when the king of Israel had read the letter, that he rent his clothes, and said, Am I God, to kill and to make alive, that this man doth send unto me to recover a man of his leprosy? but consider, I pray you, and see how he seeketh a quarrel against me. And it was so, when Elisha the man of God heard that the king of Israel had rent his clothes, that he sent to the king, saying, Wherefore hast thou rent thy clothes? let him come now to me, and he shall know that there is a prophet in Israel. So Naaman came with his horses and with his chariots, and stood at the door of the house of Elisha. And Elisha sent a messenger unto him, saying, Go and wash in Jordan seven times, and thy flesh shall come again to thee, and thou shalt be clean. But Naaman was wroth, and went away, and said, Behold, I thought, He will surely come out to me, and stand, and call on the name of the LORD his God, and wave his hand over the place, and recover the leper. Are not Abanah and Pharpar, the rivers of Damascus, better than all the waters of Israel? may I not wash in them, and be clean? So he turned and went away in a rage. And his servants came near, and spake unto him, and said, My father, if the prophet had bid thee do some great thing, wouldest thou not have done it ? how much rather then, when he saith to thee, Wash, and be clean ? Then went he down, and dipped himself seven times in Jordan, according to the saying of the man of God: and his flesh came again like unto the flesh of a little child, and he was clean. And he returned to the man of God, he and all his company, and came, and stood before him: and he said, Behold now, I know that there is no God in all the earth, but in Israel: now therefore, I pray thee, take a present of thy servant. But he said, As the LORD liveth, before whom I stand, I will receive none. And he urged him to take it; but he refused. And Naaman said, If not, yet I pray thee let there be given to thy servant two mules' burden of earth; for thy servant will henceforth offer neither burnt offering nor sacrifice unto other gods, but unto the LORD. In this thing the LORD pardon thy servant; when my master goeth into the house of Rimmon to worship there, and he leaneth on my hand, and I bow myself in the house of Rimmon, when I bow myself in the house of Rimmon, the LORD pardon thy servant in this thing. And he said unto him, Go in peace. So he departed from him a little way.

But Gehazi, the servant of Elisha the man of God, said, Behold, my master hath spared this Naaman the Syrian, in not receiving at his hands that which he brought: as the LORD liveth, I will run after him, and take somewhat of him. So Gehazi followed after Naaman. And when Naaman saw one running after him, he lighted down from the chariot to meet him, and said, Is all well? And he said, All is well. My master hath sent me, saying, Behold, even now there be come to me from the hill country of Ephraim two young men of the sons of the prophets; give them, I pray thee, a talent of silver, and two changes of raiment. And Naaman said, Be content, take two talents. And he urged him, and bound two talents of silver in two bags, with two changes of raiment, and laid them upon two of his servants; and they bare them before him. And when he came to the hill, he took them from their hand, and bestowed them in the house: and he let the men go, and they departed. But he went in, and stood before his master. And Elisha said unto him, Whence comest thou, Gehazi? And he said, Thy servant went no whither. And he said unto him, Went not mine heart with thee, when the man turned again from his chariot to meet thee? Is it a time to receive money, and to receive garments, and oliveyards and vineyards, and sheep and oxen, and menservants and maidservants? The leprosy therefore of Naaman shall cleave unto thee, and unto thy seed for ever. And he went out from his presence a leper as white as snow.

Kings and Prophets & Isaiah

vii

The Assyrian Army and the Prophet Isaiah

Now in the fourteenth year of king Hezekiah did Sennacherib king of Assyria come up against all the fenced cities of Judah, and took them.

And the king of Assyria sent Tartan and Rabsaris and Rabshakeh to king Hezekiah with a great army into Jerusalem. And they went up and came to Jerusalem. And when they were come up, they came and stood by the conduit of the upper pool, which is in the high way of the fuller's field. And when they had called to the king, there came out to them Eliakim, which was over the household, and Shebna the scribe, and Joah the son of Asaph the recorder. And Rabshakeh said unto them, Say ye now to Hezekiah, Thus saith the great king, the king of Assyria, What confidence is this wherein thou trustest? Thou sayest, but they are but vain words, There is counsel and strength for the war. Now on whom dost thou trust, that thou hast rebelled against me? Now, behold, thou trustest upon the staff of this bruised reed, even upon Egypt; whereon if a man lean, it will go into his hand, and pierce it: so is Pharaoh king of Egypt unto all that trust on him. But if ye say unto me, We trust in the LORD our God: is not that he, whose high places and whose altars Hezekiah hath taken away, and hath said to Judah and to Jerusalem, Ye shall worship before this altar in Jerusalem? ՝ Now therefore, I pray thee, give pledges to my master the king of Assyria, and I will give thee two thousand horses, if thou be able on thy part to set riders upon them. How then canst thou turn away the face of one captain of the least of my master's servants, and put thy trust on Egypt for chariots and for horsemen? Am I now come up without the LORD against this place to destroy it? The LORD said unto me, Go up against this land, and destroy it.

Then said Eliakim the son of Hilkiah, and Shebna, and Joah, unto Rabshakeh, Speak, I pray thee, to thy servants in the Syrian language; for we understand it: and speak not with us in the Jews' language, in the ears of the people that are on the wall. But Rabshakeh said unto them, Hath my master sent me to thy master, and to thee, to speak these words? hath he not sent me to the men which sit on the wall? Then Rabshakeh stood, and cried with a loud voice in the Jews' language, and spake, saying, Hear ye the word of the great king, the king of Assyria. Thus saith the king, Let not Hezekiah deceive you; for he shall not be able to deliver you out of his hand: neither let Hezekiah make you trust in the LORD, saying, The LORD will surely deliver us, and this city shall not be given into the hand of the king of Assyria. Hearken not to Hezekiah: for thus saith the king of Assyria, Make your peace with me, and come out to me; and eat ye every one of his vine, and every one of his fig tree, and drink ye every one the waters of his own cistern; until I come and take you away to a land like your own land, a land of corn and wine, a land of bread and vineyards, a land of oil olive and of honey, that ye may live, and not die: and hearken not unto Hezekiah, when he persuadeth you, saying, The LORD will deliver us. Hath any of the gods of the nations ever delivered his land out of the hand of the king of Assyria? Who are they among all the gods of the countries, that have delivered their country out of my hand, that the LORD should deliver Jerusalem out of my hand? But the people held their peace, and answered him not a word: for the king's commandment was, saying, Answer him not. Then came Eliakim the son of Hilkiah, which was over the household, and Shebna the scribe, and Joah the son of Asaph the recorder, to Hezekiah with their clothes rent, and told him the words of Rabshakeh.

And it came to pass, when king Hezekiah heard it, that he rent his clothes, and covered himself with sackcloth, and went into the house of the LORD. And he sent Eliakim, which was over the household, and Shebna the scribe, and the elders of the priests, covered with sackcloth, unto Isaiah the prophet the son of Amoz. And they said unto him, Thus saith Hezekiah, This day is a day of trouble, and of rebuke, and of contumely. It may be the LORD thy God will hear all the words of Rabshakeh, whom the king of Assyria his master hath sent to reproach the living God, and will rebuke the words which the LORD thy God hath heard: wherefore lift up thy prayer for the remnant that is left. So the servants of king Hezekiah came to Isaiah. And Isaiah said unto them, Thus shall ye say to your master, Thus saith the LORD, Be not afraid of the words that thou hast heard, wherewith the servants of the king of Assyria have blasphemed me. Behold, I will put a spirit in him, and he shall hear a rumour, and shall return to his own land; and I will cause him to fall by the sword in his own land.

So Rabshakeh returned, and found the king of Assyria warring against Libnah. And when he heard say of Tirhakah king of Ethiopia, Behold, he is come out to fight against thee: he sent messengers again unto Hezekiah, saying, Thus shall ye speak to Hezekiah king of Judah, saying, Let not thy God in whom thou trustest deceive thee, saying, Jerusalem shall not be given into the hand of the king of Assyria. Behold, thou hast heard what the kings of Assyria have done to all lands, by destroying them utterly: and shalt thou be delivered? Have the gods of the nations delivered them, which my fathers have destroyed? And Hezekiah received the letter from the hand of the messengers, and read it: and Hezekiah went up unto the house of the LORD, and spread it before the LORD. And Hezekiah prayed before the LORD, and said,

Kings and Prophets ❦   Isaiah

O LORD, the God of Israel, that sittest upon the cherubim, thou art the God, even thou alone, of all the kingdoms of the earth; thou hast made heaven and earth. Incline thine ear, O LORD, and hear; open thine eyes, O LORD, and see: and hear the words of Sennacherib, wherewith he hath sent him to reproach the living God. Of a truth, LORD, the kings of Assyria have laid waste the nations and their lands, and have cast their gods into the fire: for they were no gods, but the work of men's hands, wood and stone: therefore they have destroyed them. Now therefore, O LORD our God, save thou us, I beseech thee, out of his hand, that all the kingdoms of the earth may know that thou art the LORD God, even thou only.

Then Isaiah the son of Amoz sent to Hezekiah, saying, Thus saith the LORD, the God of Israel, Whereas thou hast prayed to me against Sennacherib king of Assyria, I have heard thee. This is the word that the LORD hath spoken concerning him: The virgin daughter of Zion hath despised thee and laughed thee to scorn; the daughter of Jerusalem hath shaken her head at thee. Whom hast thou reproached and blasphemed? and against whom hast thou exalted thy voice and lifted up thine eyes on high? even against the Holy One of Israel. By thy messengers thou hast reproached the Lord, and hast said, 'With the multitude of my chariots am I come up to the height of the mountains, to the innermost parts of Lebanon; and I will cut down the tall cedars thereof, and the choice fir trees thereof. I have digged and drunk strange waters, and with the sole of my feet will I dry up all the rivers of Egypt.' Hast thou not heard how I have done it long ago? now have I brought it to pass, that thou shouldest be to lay waste fenced cities into ruinous heaps. Therefore their inhabitants were of small power, they were dismayed and confounded; they were as the grass of the field, and as the green herb, as the grass on the housetops, and as corn blasted before it be grown up. But I know thy sitting down, and thy going out, and thy coming in, and thy raging against me. Because of thy raging against me, and for that thine arrogancy is come up into mine ears, therefore will I put my hook in thy nose, and my bridle in thy lips, and I will turn thee back by the way by which thou camest. Therefore thus saith the LORD concerning the king of Assyria, He shall not come unto this city, nor shoot an arrow there, neither shall he come before it with shield, nor cast a mount against it. By the way that he came, by the same shall he return, and he shall not come unto this city, saith the LORD. For I will defend this city to save it, for mine own sake, and for my servant David's sake.

And it came to pass that night, that the angel of the LORD went forth, and smote in the camp of the Assyrians an hundred fourscore and five thousand: and when men arose early in the morning, behold, they were all dead corpses. So Sennacherib king of Assyria departed, and went and returned, and dwelt at Nineveh. And it came to pass, as he was worshipping in the house of Nisroch his god, that Adrammelech and Sharezer smote him with the sword: and they escaped into the land of Ararat.

viii

Josiah and the Finding of the Law

And it came to pass in the eighteenth year of king Josiah, that the king sent Shaphan the scribe, to the house of the LORD, saying, Go up to Hilkiah the high priest, that he may sum the money which is brought into the house of the LORD, which the keepers of the door have gathered of the people: and let them deliver it into the hand of the workmen that have the oversight of the house of the LORD. And Hilkiah the high priest said unto Shaphan the scribe, I have found the book of the law in the house of the LORD. And Hilkiah delivered the book to Shaphan, and he read it. And Shaphan the scribe came to the king, and brought the king word again, and said, Thy servants have emptied out the money that was found in the house, and have delivered it into the hand of the workmen that have the oversight of the house of the LORD. And Shaphan the scribe told the king, saying, Hilkiah the priest hath delivered me a book. And Shaphan read it before the king. And it came to pass, when the king had heard the words of the book of the law, that he rent his clothes. And the king commanded, saying, Go ye, inquire of the LORD for me, and for the people, and for all Judah, concerning the words of this book that is found: for great is the wrath of the LORD that is kindled against us, because our fathers have not hearkened unto the words of this book, to do according unto all that which is written concerning us. So Hilkiah, and they whom the king commanded, went unto Huldah the prophetess, (now she dwelt in Jerusalem in the second quarter;) and they communed with her. And she said unto them, Thus saith the LORD, the God of Israel: Tell ye the man that sent you unto me, Thus saith the LORD, Behold, I will bring evil upon this place, and upon the inhabitants thereof, even all the words of the book which the king of Judah hath read: because they have forsaken me, and have burned incense unto other gods, that they might provoke me to anger with all the work of their hands; therefore my wrath shall be kindled against this place, and it shall not be quenched. But unto the king of Judah, who sent you to inquire of the LORD, thus shall ye say to him, Thus saith the LORD, the God of Israel: As touching the words which thou hast heard, because thine heart was tender, and thou didst humble thyself before the LORD, when thou heardest what I spake against this place, and against the inhabitants thereof, that they should become a desolation and a curse, and hast rent thy clothes, and wept before me; I also have heard thee, saith the LORD. Therefore, behold, I will gather thee to thy fathers, and thou shalt be gathered to thy grave in peace, neither shall thine eyes see all the evil which I will bring upon this place. And they brought the king word again.

And the king sent, and they gathered unto him all the elders of Judah and of Jerusalem. And the king went up to the house of the LORD, and all the men of Judah and all the inhabitants of Jerusalem with him, and the priests, and the prophets, and all the people, both small and great: and he read in their ears all the words of the book of the covenant which was found in the house of the LORD. And the king stood by the pillar, and made a covenant before the LORD, to walk after the LORD, and to keep his commandments, and his testimonies, and his statutes, with all his heart, and all his soul, to confirm the words of this covenant that were written in this book: and all the people stood to the covenant. And the inhabitants of Jerusalem did according to the covenant of God, the God of their fathers. And Josiah took away all the abominations out of all the countries that pertained to the children of Israel, and made all that were found in Israel to serve, even to serve the LORD their God. All his days they departed not from following the LORD, the God of their fathers.

Notes to the Kings and Prophets

ii. There are two messengers at the end of this story. One is the son of an eminent priest, who happens to be a swift runner; the other (the Cushite, or Ethiopian) is a servant, a professional runner. Joab is unwilling to let his friend Ahimaaz take the news on this occasion, because he foresaw it would be unwelcome to the king.

iii. All that in modern times is called science, or philosophy, was called 'wisdom' by the Hebrews. Solomon was the most eminent of the wise men of Israel, and they looked up to him as the founder of Hebrew wisdom.

iv. *To your tents, O Israel*, was the regular cry for starting a revolt among the Israelites.

v. *Baal* (sometimes used in the plural form, *the Baalim*) was an idol god, or group of idol gods, worshipped in the great merchant cities of Tyre and Zidon. Introduced into Israel by this Zidonian queen Jezebel, they proved the most dangerous of all the forms of idolatry which corrupted the worship of the Israelites. — *The Asherah* (also plural) were images used in this or similar idolatrous worship. — *The prophets of Baal — they prophesied until the time of the offering*, etc.: the literal meaning of *prophet* is *interpreter*, one who interprets for a god. As the prophets often accompanied their inspired utterances with dancing, or violent gestures, these gestures of the prophets of Baal are here spoken of as *prophesying*. — *Sons of Belial:* a common expression for vile persons, Belial being the vilest of all idol gods. — **Page 228.** *Go . . . thou shalt anoint Hazael*, etc. To understand the point of this Divine message it is necessary to remember who the prophets were. They were representatives of the original idea that the invisible God was the ruler of Israel; the kings being tolerated only so long as they faithfully represented him. Thus in God's commission to Elijah he is resuming his rule of Israel, by ordering the prophet to anoint, in place of the wicked Ahab, a king who would overthrow Baal worshippers with a violence as great as their own. Further, as Elijah had been depressed by the thought of his solitariness, he is commissioned to name a successor to carry on the prophetic work when he is no more. — **Page 233.** *Let a double portion of thy spirit be upon me:* the double portion was the eldest son's inheritance; Elisha petitions to be in this way the foremost successor of his master.

vi. Page 239. *Two mules' burden of earth.* The idea of heathen nations at this time was that a god was a local being, having power only in the country where he was worshipped. Thus Naaman, wishing from gratitude to worship Israel's God, supposed it necessary to have a portion of Israel's land, enough to erect an altar upon. — *The house of Rimmon:* Rimmon was the chief idol god worshipped by the Syrians.

vii. *Tartan and Rabsaris and Rabshakeh:* these are not names of persons, but titles of offices in the Assyrian army and court. We should say *the Rabshakeh*. — **Page 241.** *We trust in the* LORD *. . . is not that he whose high places and altars Hezekiah hath taken away?* The worship *in the high places* (mountain groves) was only in name a worship of the LORD, it was really a cover for idolatrous and wicked rites. Hezekiah had been fulfilling the law in putting it down. But the Assyrian officer either misunderstands this, or purposely uses it to frighten the Jews with the idea that the king has offended God. — **Page 245.** *O LORD . . . that sittest upon the Cherubim.* This is a reference to the Ark, which was the symbol of the Divine presence. Its cover was called, The Mercy-seat, and on it were figures of angels, or cherubim, whose outspread wings covered the whole Mercy-seat. — **Page 246.** *Hast thou not heard how I have done it long ago?* The point of Isaiah's words to the Assyrians is this: that all the victorious career of which the Assyrian was so proud was simply the LORD's way of using him as his own instrument to punish the wicked. — Psalms 46, 48, 76, were composed in commemoration of this overthrow of Sennacherib.

 viii. *I have found the book of the law.* What exactly was the book found on this occasion we do not know: but it is certain that the portion of the Bible called *Deuteronomy* was either the whole or a part of what was discovered, and it was this which produced the great impression.

BIBLE STORIES

THE EXILE AND RETURN

INTRODUCTION TO THE EXILE AND RETURN

At the close of the last period both the kingdoms of Judah and Israel had been carried away into captivity. Something like seventy years elapsed before there was any sign of their deliverance; and during this period their Babylonian conquerors were themselves conquered by the Medes and Persians. But meanwhile the history of the Hebrew people is not entirely lost: certain stories preserved in other parts of Scripture give us a glimpse of the exiles in their land of captivity.

These stories of the Exile are amongst the most famous stories in all literature. One group of them has for its heroes Daniel and three less distinguished companions of his, who were all carried together into Babylon. This Babylon was the chief city of the Chaldeans, a people distinguished among the nations of antiquity for 'soothsaying,' or the power of reading the future by the stars or other means. By the aid of God Daniel and his companions were able to surpass the Chaldeans in their own art; they thus were raised to the highest positions in the empire. Alike when they were lowly and when they were exalted, all efforts to shake their fidelity to the worship of their fathers' God proved vain. Thus by the agency of Daniel and his fellows the Chosen Nation even in its captivity was enabled to continue its mission of witnessing for God to the nations.

As the men of the Exile are represented by Daniel and his companions, so we have a picture of the women in the beautiful Story of Esther. Who exactly is the monarch alluded to under the name Ahasuerus it is difficult to determine; but his empire is said to consist of a hundred and twenty-seven provinces, with Jews scattered through them all. Esther was a girl chosen for her beauty, after the empire had been searched through and through, to become the queen of Ahasuerus. She had not told her Jewish birth; and her cousin Mordecai, who had brought her up from childhood, remained amongst the humbler courtiers to watch over her safety. By the skill of this Mordecai, and the royal position of Esther, she was enabled, though at the risk of her life, to avert a dreadful blow aimed at the Jews throughout the empire, by which it had been intended to destroy the whole race. Mordecai became prime minister of the empire, and the deliverance was celebrated by an annual feast of the Jews.

At last came the Return from Captivity. This was not a single incident, but a series of migrations, by which successive bands of exiles were permitted to return to the holy land, and set up again the worship of God. The effect of the Exile was to sift for ever the earnest worshippers of God from the Israelites who were inclined to

Exile and Return   Introduction

idolatry; only the former would care to return to Palestine, and the restored community was not the Hebrew nation but the Jewish Church. The chief names connected with the Return are Ezra and Nehemiah. The portion of Scripture entitled The Chronicles *was the production of this restored Jewish Church, and contains the documents throwing light upon the Return from Exile. One story here given is Nehemiah's description of his journey from Babylon and the rebuilding of the walls of Jerusalem. The account of the Renewal of the Covenant, under Ezra and Nehemiah, between God and his restored people, and the prayer in which the whole history of Israel is reviewed, make an appropriate close for a series of Old Testament stories.*

STORIES FROM THE EXILE AND RETURN

i. Stories of the Captives in Babylon
   The Burning Fiery Furnace
   The Dream of the Tree that was cut down
   Belshazzar's Feast
   Daniel in the Den of Lions

ii. The Story of Esther
   How a Jewish Maiden became a Queen
   Haman's Wicked Plot and how it was overthrown
   Mordecai Prime Minister of the Empire

iii. Stories of the Return
   How Nehemiah rebuilt the Walls of Jerusalem
   The Renewal of the Covenant under Ezra

i

Stories of the Captives in Babylon

The Burning Fiery Furnace

Nebuchadnezzar the king made an image of gold, whose height was threescore cubits, and the breadth thereof six cubits: he set it up in the plain of Dura, in the province of Babylon. Then Nebuchadnezzar the king sent to gather together the satraps, the deputies, and the governors, the judges, the treasurers, the counsellors, the sheriffs, and all the rulers of the provinces, to come to the dedication of the image which Nebuchadnezzar the king had set up. Then the satraps, the deputies, and the governors, the judges, the treasurers, the counsellors, the sheriffs, and all the rulers of the provinces, were gathered together unto the dedication of the image that Nebuchadnezzar the king had set up; and they stood before the image that Nebuchadnezzar had set up. Then the herald cried aloud, To you it is commanded, O peoples, nations, and languages, that at what time ye hear the sound of the cornet, flute, harp, sackbut, psaltery, dulcimer, and all kinds of music, ye fall down and worship the golden image that Nebuchadnezzar the king hath set up: and whoso falleth not down and worshippeth shall the same hour be cast into the midst of a burning fiery furnace. Therefore at that time, when all the peoples heard the sound of the cornet, flute, harp, sackbut, psaltery, and all kinds of music, all the peoples, the nations, and the languages, fell down and worshipped the golden image that Nebuchadnezzar the king had set up.

Wherefore at that time certain Chaldeans came near, and brought accusation against the Jews. They answered and said to Nebuchadnezzar the king: O king, live for ever. Thou, O king, hast made a decree, that every man that shall hear the sound of the cornet, flute, harp, sackbut, psaltery, and dulcimer, and all kinds of music, shall fall down and worship the golden image: and whoso falleth not down and worshippeth, shall be cast into the midst of a burning fiery furnace. There are certain Jews whom thou hast appointed over the affairs of the province of Babylon, Shadrach, Meshach, and Abed-nego; these men, O king, have not regarded thee: they serve not thy gods, nor worship the golden image which thou hast set up. Then Nebuchadnezzar in his rage and fury commanded to bring Shadrach, Meshach, and Abed-nego. Then they brought these men before the king. Nebuchadnezzar answered and said unto them, Is it of purpose, O Shadrach, Meshach, and Abed-nego, that ye serve not my god, nor worship the golden image which I have set up? Now if ye be ready that at what time ye hear the sound of the cornet, flute, harp, sackbut, psaltery, and dulcimer, and all kinds of music, ye fall down and worship the image which I have made, well: but if ye worship not, ye shall be cast the same hour into the midst of a burning fiery furnace; and who is that god that shall deliver you out of my hands? Shadrach, Meshach, and Abed-nego, answered and said to the king, O Nebuchadnezzar, we have no need to answer thee in this matter. If it be so, our God whom we serve is able to deliver us from the burning fiery furnace; and he will deliver us out of thine hand, O king. But if not, be it known unto thee, O king, that we will not serve thy gods, nor worship the golden image which thou hast set up. Then was Nebuchadnezzar full of fury, and the form of his visage was changed against Shadrach, Meshach, and Abed-nego: therefore he spake, and commanded that they should heat the furnace seven times more than it was wont to be heated. And he commanded certain mighty men that were in his army to bind Shadrach, Meshach, and Abed-nego, and to cast them into the burning fiery furnace. Then these men were bound in their hosen, their tunics, and their mantles, and their other garments, and were cast into the midst of the burning fiery furnace. Therefore because the king's commandment was urgent, and the furnace exceeding hot, the flame of the fire slew those men that took up Shadrach, Meshach, and Abednego. And these three men, Shadrach, Meshach, and

Abed-nego, fell down bound into the midst of the burning fiery furnace.

Then Nebuchadnezzar the king was astonied, and rose up in haste: he spake and said unto his counsellors, Did not we cast three men bound into the midst of the fire? They answered and said unto the king, True, O king. He answered and said, Lo, I see four men loose, walking in the midst of the fire, and they have no hurt; and the aspect of the fourth is like a son of the gods. Then Nebuchadnezzar came near to the mouth of the burning fiery furnace: he spake and said, Shadrach, Meshach, and Abed-nego, ye servants of the Most High God, come forth, and come hither. Then Shadrach, Meshach, and Abed-nego, came forth out of the midst of the fire. And the satraps, the deputies, and the governors, and the king's counsellors, being gathered together, saw these men, that the fire had no power upon their bodies, nor was the hair of their head singed, neither were their hosen changed, nor had the smell of fire passed on them. Nebuchadnezzar spake and said: Blessed be the God of Shadrach, Meshach, and Abed-nego, who hath sent his angel, and delivered his servants that trusted in him, and have changed the king's word, and have yielded their bodies, that they might not serve nor worship any god, except their own God. Therefore I make a decree, that every people, nation, and language, which speak any thing amiss against the God of Shadrach, Meshach, and Abed-nego, shall be cut in pieces,

Exile and Return   Daniel

and their houses shall be made a dunghill: because there is no other god that is able to deliver after this sort. Then the king promoted Shadrach, Meshach, and Abednego, in the province of Babylon.

The Dream of the Tree that was cut down

'Nebuchadnezzar the king, unto all the peoples, nations, and languages, that dwell in all the earth: peace be multiplied unto you. It hath seemed good unto me to shew the signs and wonders that the Most High God hath wrought toward me. How great are his signs! and how mighty are his wonders! his kingdom is an everlasting kingdom, and his dominion is from generation to generation.

'I Nebuchadnezzar was at rest in mine house, and flourishing in my palace. I saw a dream which made me afraid; and the thoughts upon my bed and the visions of my head troubled me. Therefore made I a decree to bring in all the wise men of Babylon before me, that they might make known unto me the interpretation of the dream. Then came in the magicians, the enchanters, the Chaldeans, and the soothsayers: and I told the dream before them; but they did not make known unto me the interpretation thereof. But at the last Daniel came in before me, whose name was Belteshazzar, according to the name of my god, and in whom is the spirit of the holy gods: and I told the dream before him, saying, O Belteshazzar, master of the magicians, because I know that the spirit of the holy gods is in thee, and no secret troubleth thee, tell me the visions of my dream that I have seen, and the interpretation thereof.

'Thus were the visions of my head upon my bed: I saw, and behold a tree in the midst of the earth, and the height thereof was great. The tree grew, and was strong, and the height thereof reached unto heaven, and the sight thereof to the end of all the earth. The leaves thereof were fair, and the fruit thereof much, and in it was meat for all: the beasts of the field had shadow under it, and the fowls of the heaven dwelt in the branches thereof, and all flesh was fed of it. I saw in the visions of my head upon my bed, and, behold, a watcher and an holy one came down from heaven. He cried aloud, and said thus: "Hew down the tree, and cut off his branches, shake off his leaves, and scatter his fruit: let the beasts get away from under it, and the fowls from his branches. Nevertheless leave the stump of his roots in the earth, even with a band of iron and brass, in the tender grass of the field; and let it be wet with the dew of heaven, and let his portion be with the beasts in the grass of the earth: let his heart be changed from man's, and let a beast's heart be given unto him; and let seven times pass over him: to the intent that the living may know that the Most High ruleth in the kingdom of men, and giveth it to whomsoever he will, and setteth up over it the lowest of men." This dream I king Nebuchadnezzar have seen: and thou, O Belteshazzar, declare the interpretation, forasmuch as all the wise men of my kingdom are not able to make known unto me the interpretation; but thou art able, for the spirit of the holy gods is in thee.

'Then Daniel, whose name was Belteshazzar, was astonied for a while, and his thoughts troubled him. The king answered and said, Belteshazzar, let not the dream, or the interpretation, trouble thee. Belteshazzar answered and said, My lord, the dream be to them that hate thee, and the interpretation thereof to thine adversaries. The tree that thou sawest, which grew, and was strong, whose height reached unto the heaven, and the sight thereof to all the earth; whose leaves were fair, and the fruit thereof much, and in it was meat for all; under which the beasts of the field dwelt, and upon whose branches the fowls of the heaven had their habitation; it is thou, O king, that art grown and become strong: for thy greatness is grown, and reacheth unto heaven, and thy dominion to the end of the earth. And whereas the king saw a watcher and an holy one coming down from heaven, and saying, Hew down the tree, and destroy it; nevertheless leave the stump of the roots thereof in the earth, even with a band of iron and brass, in the tender grass of the field; and let it be wet with the dew of heaven, and let his portion be with the beasts of the field, till seven times pass over him;

this is the interpretation, O king, and it is the decree of the Most High, which is come upon my lord the king: that thou shalt be driven from men, and thy dwelling shall be with the beasts of the field, and thou shalt be made to eat grass as oxen, and shalt be wet with the dew of heaven, and seven times shall pass over thee; till thou know that the Most High ruleth in the kingdom of men, and giveth it to whomsoever he will. And whereas they commanded to leave the stump of the tree roots; thy kingdom shall be sure unto thee, after that thou shalt have known that the heavens do rule. Wherefore, O king, let my counsel be acceptable unto thee, and break off thy sins by righteousness, and thine iniquities by shewing mercy to the poor; if there may be a lengthening of thy tranquillity.

'All this came upon the king Nebuchadnezzar. At the end of twelve months he was walking in the royal palace of Babylon. The king spake and said, Is not this great Babylon, which I have built for the royal dwelling place, by the might of my power and for the glory of my majesty? While the word was in the king's mouth, there fell a voice from heaven, saying: "O king Nebuchadnezzar, to thee it is spoken: the kingdom is departed from thee. And thou shalt be driven from men, and thy dwelling shall be with the beasts of the field; thou shalt be made to eat grass as oxen, and seven times shall pass over thee; until thou know that the Most High ruleth in the kingdom of men, and giveth it to whomsoever he will." The same hour was the thing fulfilled upon Nebuchadnezzar: and he was driven from men, and did eat grass as oxen, and his body was wet with the dew of heaven, till his hair was grown like eagles' feathers, and his nails like birds' claws. And at the end of the days I Nebuchadnezzar lifted up mine eyes unto heaven, and mine understanding returned unto me, and I blessed the Most High, and I praised and honoured him that liveth for ever; for his dominion is an everlasting dominion, and his kingdom from generation to generation: and all the inhabitants of the earth are reputed as nothing: and he doeth according to his will in the army of heaven, and among the inhabitants of the earth: and none can stay his hand, or say unto him, What doest thou? At the same time mine understanding returned unto me; and for the glory of my kingdom, my majesty and brightness returned unto me; and my counsellors and my lords sought unto me; and I was established in my kingdom, and excellent greatness was added unto me.

'Now I Nebuchadnezzar praise and extol and honour the King of heaven; for all his works are truth, and his ways judgement: and those that walk in pride he is able to abase.'

Belshazzar's Feast

Belshazzar the king made a great feast to a thousand of his lords, and drank wine before the thousand. Belshazzar, whiles he tasted the wine, commanded to bring the golden and silver vessels which Nebuchadnezzar his father had taken out of the temple which was in Jerusalem; that the king and his lords might drink therein. Then they brought the golden vessels that were taken out of the temple of the house of God which was at Jerusalem; and the king and his lords drank in them. They drank wine, and praised the gods of gold, and of silver, of brass, of iron, of wood, and of stone. In the same hour came forth the fingers of a man's hand, and wrote over against the candlestick upon the plaister of the wall of the king's palace: and the king saw the part of the hand that wrote. Then the king's countenance was changed in him, and his thoughts troubled him; and the joints of his loins were loosed, and his knees smote one against another. The king cried aloud to bring in the enchanters, the Chaldeans, and the soothsayers. The king spake and said to the wise men of Babylon, Whosoever shall read this writing, and shew me the interpretation thereof, shall be clothed with purple, and have a chain of gold about his neck, and shall rule as one of three in the kingdom. Then came in all the king's wise men: but they could not read the writing, nor make

Exile and Return — Daniel

known to the king the interpretation. Then was king Belshazzar greatly troubled, and his countenance was changed in him, and his lords were perplexed.

Now the queen by reason of the words of the king and his lords came into the banquet house: the queen spake and said: O king, live for ever; let not thy thoughts trouble thee, nor let thy countenance be changed: there is a man in thy kingdom, in whom is the spirit of the holy gods; and in the days of thy father light and understanding and wisdom, like the wisdom of the gods, was found in him: and the king Nebuchadnezzar thy father, the king, I say, thy father, made him master of the magicians, enchanters, Chaldeans, and soothsayers; forasmuch as an excellent spirit, and knowledge, and understanding, interpreting of dreams, and shewing of dark sentences, and dissolving of doubts, were found in the same Daniel, whom the king named Belteshazzar. Now let Daniel be called, and he will shew the interpretation.

Then was Daniel brought in before the king. The king spake and said unto Daniel, Art thou that Daniel, which art of the children of the captivity of Judah, whom the king my father brought out of Judah? I have heard of thee, that the spirit of the gods is in thee, and that light and understanding and excellent wisdom is found in thee. And now the wise men, the enchanters, have been brought in before me, that they should read this writing, and make known unto me the interpretation thereof: but they could not shew the interpretation of the thing. But I have heard of thee, that thou canst give interpretations, and dissolve doubts: now if thou canst read the writing, and make known to me the interpretation thereof, thou shalt be clothed with purple, and have a chain of gold about thy neck, and shalt rule as one of three in the kingdom. Then Daniel answered and said before the king: Let thy gifts be to thyself, and give thy rewards to another; nevertheless I will read the writing unto the king, and make known to him the interpretation. O thou king, the Most High God gave Nebuchadnezzar thy father the kingdom, and greatness, and glory, and majesty: and because of the greatness that he gave him, all the peoples, nations, and languages trembled and feared before him: whom he would he slew, and whom he would he kept alive; and whom he would he raised up, and whom he would he put down. But when his heart was lifted up, and his spirit was hardened that he dealt proudly, he was deposed from his kingly throne, and they took his glory from him: and he was driven from the sons of men; and his heart was made like the beasts, and his dwelling was with the wild asses; he was fed with grass like oxen, and his body was wet with the dew of heaven: until he knew that the Most High God ruleth in the kingdom of men, and that he setteth up over it whomsoever he will. And thou his son, O Belshazzar, hast not humbled thine heart, though thou knewest all this: but hast lifted up thyself

Exile and Return — Daniel

against the Lord of heaven; and they have brought the vessels of his house before thee, and thou and thy lords have drunk wine in them; and thou hast praised the gods of silver, and gold, of brass, iron, wood, and stone, which see not, nor hear, nor know: and the God in whose hand thy breath is, and whose are all thy ways, hast thou not glorified: then was the part of the hand sent from before him, and this writing was inscribed. And this is the writing that was inscribed*:

M	U	P
E	L	H
N	E	A
E	K	R
M	E	S
E	T	I
N	E	N

This is the interpretation of the thing: —

MENE

God hath NUMBERED thy kingdom:
And brought it to an end!

TEKEL

Thou art WEIGHED in the balances:
And art found wanting!

[* Daniel reads down, up, down: instead of across.]

PERES

Thy kingdom is DIVIDED:
And given to the Medes and Persians!

Then commanded Belshazzar, and they clothed Daniel with purple, and put a chain of gold about his neck, and made proclamation concerning him, that he should rule as one of three in the kingdom. In that night Belshazzar the Chaldean king was slain, and Darius the Mede received the kingdom.

Daniel in the Den of Lions

It pleased Darius to set over the kingdom an hundred and twenty satraps, which should be throughout the whole kingdom; and over them three presidents, of whom Daniel was one; that these satraps might give account unto them, and that the king should have no damage. Then this Daniel was distinguished above the presidents and the satraps, because an excellent spirit was in him; and the king thought to set him over the whole realm.

Then the presidents and the satraps sought to find occasion against Daniel as touching the kingdom; but they could find none occasion nor fault; forasmuch as he was faithful, neither was there any error or fault found in him. Then said these men, We shall not find any occasion against this Daniel, except we find it against him concerning the law of his God. Then these presidents and satraps assembled together to the king, and said thus unto him: King Darius, live for ever. All the presidents of the kingdom, the deputies and the satraps, the counsellors and the governors, have consulted together to establish a royal statute, and to make a strong interdict, that whosoever shall ask a petition of any god or man for thirty days, save of thee, O king, he shall be cast into the den of lions. Now, O king, establish the interdict, and sign the writing, that it be not changed, according to the law of the Medes and Persians, which altereth not. Wherefore king Darius signed the writing and the interdict.

And when Daniel knew that the writing was signed, he went into his house; (now his windows were open in his chamber toward Jerusalem;) and he kneeled upon his knees three times a day, and prayed, and gave thanks before his God, as he did aforetime. Then these men assembled together, and found Daniel making petition and supplication before his God. Then they came near, and spake before the king concerning the king's interdict: Hast thou not signed an interdict, that every man that shall make petition unto any god or man within thirty days, save unto thee, O king, shall be cast into the den of lions? The king answered and said, The thing is true, according to the law of the Medes and Persians, which altereth not. Then answered they and said before the king, That Daniel, which is of the children of the captivity of Judah, regardeth not thee, O king, nor the interdict that thou hast signed, but maketh his petition three times a day. Then the king, when he heard these words, was sore displeased, and set his heart on Daniel to deliver him: and he laboured till the going down of the sun to rescue him. Then these men assembled together unto the king, and said unto the king, Know, O king, that it is a law of the Medes and Persians, that no interdict nor statute which the king establisheth may be changed. Then the king commanded, and they brought Daniel and cast him into the den of lions. Now the king spake and said unto Daniel, Thy God whom thou servest continually, he will deliver thee. And a stone was brought, and laid upon the mouth of the den; and the king sealed it with his own signet, and with the signet of his lords; that nothing might be changed concerning Daniel.

Then the king went to his palace, and passed the night fasting; neither were instruments of music brought before him; and his sleep fled from him. Then the king arose very early in the morning, and went in haste unto the den of lions. And when he came near unto the den to Daniel, he cried with a lamentable voice: the king spake and said to Daniel, O Daniel, servant of the living God, is thy God, whom thou servest continually, able to deliver thee from the lions? Then said Daniel unto the king, O king, live for ever. My God hath sent his angel, and hath shut the lions' mouths, and they have not hurt me:

forasmuch as before him innocency was found in me; and also before thee, O king, have I done no hurt. Then was the king exceeding glad and commanded that they should take Daniel up out of the den. So Daniel was taken up out of the den, and no manner of hurt was found upon him, because he had trusted in his God. And the king commanded, and they brought those men which had accused Daniel, and they cast them into the den of lions, them, their children, and their wives; and the lions had the mastery of them, and brake all their bones in pieces, or ever they came at the bottom of the den.

ii

The Story of Esther

How a Jewish Maiden became a Queen

Now it came to pass in the days of Ahasuerus, (this is Ahasuerus which reigned, from India even unto Ethiopia, over an hundred and seven and twenty provinces:) that in those days, when the king Ahasuerus sat on the throne of his kingdom, which was in Shushan the palace, in the third year of his reign, he made a feast unto all his princes and his servants; the power of Persia and Media, the nobles and princes of the provinces, being before him: when he shewed the riches of his glorious kingdom and the honour of his excellent majesty many days, even an hundred and fourscore days. And when these days were fulfilled, the king made a feast unto all the people that were present in Shushan the palace, both great and small, seven days, in the court of the garden of the king's palace.

On the seventh day, when the heart of the king was merry with wine, he commanded the seven chamberlains to bring Vashti the queen before the king with the crown royal, to shew the peoples and the princes her beauty: for she was fair to look on. But the queen Vashti refused to come at the king's commandment: therefore was the king very wroth, and his anger burned in him. Then the king said to the wise men, What shall we do unto the queen Vashti according to law, because she hath not done the bidding of the king Ahasuerus? And Memucan answered before the king and the princes: 'If it please the king, let there go forth a royal commandment from him, and let it be written among the laws of the Persians and the Medes that it be not altered, that Vashti come no more before king Ahasuerus; and let the king give her royal estate unto another that is better than she.' And the saying pleased the king and the princes; and the king did according to the word of Memucan.

After these things, when the wrath of king Ahasuerus

was pacified, he remembered Vashti, and what she had done, and what was decreed against her. Then said the king's servants that ministered unto him, Let there be fair young virgins sought for the king: and let the king appoint officers in all the provinces of his kingdom, that they may gather together all the fair young virgins unto Shushan the palace; and let the maiden which pleaseth the king be queen instead of Vashti. And the thing pleased the king; and he did so.

There was a certain Jew in Shushan the palace, whose name was Mordecai, a Benjamite; who had been carried away from Jerusalem with the captives which had been carried away with Jeconiah king of Judah, whom Nebuchadnezzar the king of Babylon had carried away. And he brought up Hadassah, that is, Esther, his uncle's daughter: for she had neither father nor mother, and the maiden was fair and beautiful; and when her father and mother were dead, Mordecai took her for his own daughter. So it came to pass, when the king's commandment and his decree was heard, and when many maidens were gathered together unto Shushan the palace, that Esther was taken into the king's house. And the king loved Esther above all the women, and she obtained grace and favour in his sight more than all the virgins; so that he set the royal crown upon her head, and made her queen instead of Vashti. Then the king made a great feast unto all his princes and his servants, even Esther's feast; and he made a release to the provinces, and gave gifts, according to the bounty of the king.

In those days, while Mordecai sat in the king's gate, two of the king's chamberlains, Bigthan and Teresh, of those which kept the door, were wroth, and sought to lay hands on the king Ahasuerus. And the thing was known to Mordecai, who shewed it unto Esther the queen; and Esther told the king thereof in Mordecai's name. And when inquisition was made of the matter, and it was found to be so, they were both hanged on a tree: and it was written in the book of the chronicles before the king.

Haman's Wicked Plot, and how it was Overthrown

After these things did king Ahasuerus promote Haman the Agagite, and advanced him and set his seat above all the princes that were with him. And all the king's servants, that were in the king's gate, bowed down, and did reverence to Haman: for the king had so commanded concerning him. But Mordecai bowed not down, nor did him reverence. Then the king's servants, that were in the king's gate, said unto Mordecai, Why transgressest thou the king's commandment? Now it came to pass, when they spake daily unto him, and he hearkened not unto them, that they told Haman. And when Haman saw that Mordecai bowed not down, nor did him reverence, then was Haman full of wrath. But he thought scorn to lay hands on Mordecai alone; wherefore Haman sought to destroy all the Jews that were throughout the whole kingdom of Ahasuerus, even the people of Mordecai.

And Haman said unto king Ahasuerus, There is a certain people scattered abroad and dispersed among the peoples in all the provinces of thy kingdom; and their laws are diverse from those of every people; neither keep they the king's laws: therefore it is not for the king's profit to suffer them. If it please the king, let it be written that they be destroyed: and I will pay ten thousand talents of silver into the hands of those that have the charge of the king's business, to bring it into the king's treasuries. And the king took his ring from his hand, and gave it unto Haman the Agagite, the Jews' enemy. And the king said unto Haman, The silver is given to thee, the people also, to do with them as it seemeth good to thee.

Then were the king's scribes called in the first month, on the thirteenth day thereof, and there was written according to all that Haman commanded unto the king's satraps, and to the governors that were over every province, and to the princes of every people; to every province according to the writing thereof, and to every people after their language; in the name of king Ahasuerus was it written, and it was sealed with the king's ring. And letters were sent by posts into all the king's provinces, to destroy, to slay, and to cause to perish, all Jews, both young and old, little children and women, in one day, even upon the thirteenth day of the twelfth month, which is the month Adar, and to take the spoil of them for a prey. And the king and Haman sat down to drink; but the city of Shushan was perplexed.

Now when Mordecai knew all that was done, Mordecai rent his clothes, and put on sackcloth with ashes, and went out into the midst of the city, and cried with a loud and a bitter cry: and he came even before the king's gate: for none might enter within the king's gate clothed with sackcloth. And in every province, whithersoever the king's commandment and his decree came, there was great mourning among the Jews, and fasting, and weeping, and wailing; and many lay in sackcloth and ashes. And Esther's maidens and her chamberlains came and told it her; and the queen was exceedingly grieved: and she sent raiment to clothe Mordecai, and to take his sackcloth from off him: but he received it not. Then called Esther for Hathach, one of the king's chamberlains, whom he had appointed to attend upon her, and charged him to go to Mordecai, to know what this was, and why it was. So Hathach went forth to Mordecai unto the broad place of the city, which was before the king's gate. And Mordecai told him of all that had happened unto him, and the exact sum of the money that Haman had promised to pay to the king's treasuries for the Jews, to destroy them. Also he gave him the copy of the writing of the decree that was given out in Shushan to destroy them, to shew it unto Esther, and to declare it unto her; and to charge her that she should go in unto the king, to make supplication unto him, and to make request before him, for her people. And Hathach came and told Esther the words of Mordecai. Then Esther spake unto Hathach, and gave him a message unto Mordecai, saying: All the king's servants, and the people of the king's provinces, do know, that whosoever, whether man or woman, shall come unto the king into the inner court, who is not called, there is one law for him, that he be put to death, except such to whom the king shall hold out the golden sceptre, that he may live: but I have not been called to come in unto the king these thirty days. And they told to Mordecai Esther's words. Then Mordecai bade them return answer unto Esther, Think not with thyself that thou shalt escape in the king's house, more than all the Jews. For if thou altogether holdest thy peace at this time, then shall relief and deliverance arise to the Jews from another place, but thou and thy father's house shall perish. And who knoweth whether thou art not come to the kingdom for such a time as this? Then Esther bade them return answer unto Mordecai, Go, gather together all the Jews that are present in Shushan, and fast ye for me, and neither eat nor drink three days, night or day: I also and my maidens will fast in like manner; and so will I go in unto the king, which is not according to the law: and if I perish, I perish. So Mordecai went his way, and did according to all that Esther had commanded him.

Now it came to pass on the third day, that Esther put on her royal apparel, and stood in the inner court of the king's house, over against the king's house: and the king sat upon his royal throne in the royal house, over against the entrance of the house. And it was so, when the king saw Esther the queen standing in the court, that she obtained favour in his sight: and the king held out to Esther the golden sceptre that was in his hand. So Esther drew near, and touched the top of the sceptre. Then said the king unto her, What wilt thou, queen Esther? and what is thy request? it shall be given thee even to the half of the kingdom. And Esther said, If it seem good unto the king, let the king and Haman come this day unto the banquet that I have prepared for him. Then the king said, Cause Haman to make haste, that it may be done as Esther hath said. So the king and Haman came to the banquet that Esther had prepared. And the king said unto Esther at the banquet of wine, What is thy petition? and it shall be granted thee: and what is thy request? even to the half of the kingdom it shall be performed. Then answered Esther, and said, My petition and my request is; if I have found favour in the sight of the king, and if it please the king to grant my petition, and to perform my request, let the king and Haman come to the banquet that I shall prepare for them, and I will do tomorrow as the king hath said.

Exile and Return — Esther

Then went Haman forth that day joyful and glad of heart: but when Haman saw Mordecai in the king's gate, that he stood not up nor moved for him, he was filled with wrath against Mordecai. Nevertheless Haman refrained himself, and went home; and he sent and fetched his friends and Zeresh his wife. And Haman recounted unto them the glory of his riches, and the multitude of his children, and all the things wherein the king had promoted him, and how he had advanced him above the princes and servants of the king. Haman said moreover, Yea, Esther the queen did let no man come in with the king unto the banquet that she had prepared but myself; and tomorrow also am I invited by her together with the king. Yet all this availeth me nothing, so long as I see Mordecai the Jew sitting at the king's gate. Then said Zeresh his wife and all his friends unto him, Let a gallows be made of fifty cubits high, and in the morning speak thou unto the king that Mordecai may be hanged thereon: then go thou in merrily with the king unto the banquet. And the thing pleased Haman; and he caused the gallows to be made.

On that night could not the king sleep; and he commanded to bring the book of records of the chronicles, and they were read before the king. And it was found written, that Mordecai had told of Bigthana and Teresh, two of the king's chamberlains, of those that kept the door, who had sought to lay hands on the king Ahasuerus. And the king said, What honour and dignity hath been done to Mordecai for this? Then said the king's servants that ministered unto him, There is nothing done for him. And the king said, Who is in the court? Now Haman was come into the outward court of the king's house, to speak unto the king to hang Mordecai on the gallows that he had prepared for him. And the king's servants said unto him, Behold, Haman standeth in the court. And the king said, Let him come in. So Haman came in. And the king said unto him, What shall be done unto the man whom the king delighteth to honour? Now Haman said in his heart, To whom would the king delight to do honour more than to myself? And Haman said unto the king, For the man whom the king delighteth to honour, let royal apparel be brought which the king useth to wear, and the horse that the king rideth upon, and on the head of which a crown royal is set: and let the apparel and the horse be delivered to the hand of one of the king's most noble princes, that they may array the man withal whom the king delighteth to honour, and cause him to ride on horseback through the street of the city, and proclaim before him, Thus shall it be done to the man whom the king delighteth to honour. Then the king said to Haman, Make haste, and take the apparel and the horse, as thou hast said, and do even so to Mordecai the Jew, that sitteth at the king's gate: let nothing fail of all that thou hast spoken.

Then took Haman the apparel and the horse, and arrayed Mordecai, and caused him to ride through the street of the city, and proclaimed before him, Thus shall it be done unto the man whom the king delighteth to honour. And Mordecai came again to the king's gate. But Haman hasted to his house, mourning and having his head covered. And Haman recounted unto Zeresh his wife and all his friends every thing that had befallen him. Then said his wise men and Zeresh his wife unto him, If Mordecai, before whom thou hast begun to fall, be of the seed of the Jews, thou shalt not prevail against him, but shalt surely fall before him. While they were yet talking with him, came the king's chamberlains, and hasted to bring Haman unto the banquet that Esther had prepared.

So the king and Haman came to banquet with Esther the queen. And the king said again unto Esther on the second day at the banquet of wine, What is thy petition, queen Esther? and it shall be granted thee: and what is thy request? even to the half of the kingdom it shall be performed. Then Esther the queen answered and said, If I have found favour in thy sight, O king, and if it please the king, let my life be given me at my petition, and my people at my request: for we are sold, I and my people, to be destroyed, to be slain, and to perish. But if we had been sold for bondmen and bondwomen, I had held my peace, although the adversary could not have compensated for the king's damage. Then spake the king Ahasuerus and said unto Esther the queen, Who is he, and where is he, that durst presume in his heart to do so? And Esther said, An adversary and an enemy, even this wicked Haman. Then Haman was afraid before the king and the queen. And the king arose in his wrath from the banquet of wine. Then said Harbonah, one of the chamberlains that were before the king, Behold also, the gallows fifty cubits high, which Haman hath made for Mordecai, who spake good for the king, standeth in the house of Haman. And the king said, Hang him thereon. So they hanged Haman on the gallows that he had prepared for Mordecai. Then was the king's wrath pacified.

Mordecai Prime Minister of the Empire

On that day did the king Ahasuerus give the house of Haman the Jews' enemy unto Esther the queen. And Mordecai came before the king; for Esther had told what he was unto her. And the king took off his ring, which he had taken from Haman, and gave it unto Mordecai. And Esther set Mordecai over the house of Haman. And Esther spake yet again before the king, and fell down at his feet, and besought him with tears to put away the mischief of Haman the Agagite, and his device that he had devised against the Jews. Then the king held out to Esther the golden sceptre. So Esther arose, and stood before the king. And she said, If it please the king, and if I have found favour in his sight, and the thing seem

Exile and Return — Esther

right before the king, and I be pleasing in his eyes, let it be written to reverse the letters devised by Haman the Agagite, which he wrote to destroy the Jews which are in all the king's provinces: for how can I endure to see the evil that shall come unto my people? or how can I endure to see the destruction of my kindred? Then the king Ahasuerus said unto Esther the queen and to Mordecai the Jew, Behold, I have given Esther the house of Haman, and him they have hanged upon the gallows, because he laid his hand upon the Jews. Write ye also to the Jews, as it liketh you, in the king's name, and seal it with the king's ring: for the writing which is written in the king's name, and sealed with the king's ring, may no man reverse.

Then were the king's scribes called at that time, in the third month, which is the month Sivan, on the three and twentieth day thereof; and it was written according to all that Mordecai commanded unto the Jews, and to the satraps, and the governors and princes of the provinces which are from India unto Ethiopia, an hundred twenty and seven provinces, unto every province according to the writing thereof, and unto every people after their language, and to the Jews according to their writing, and according to their language. And he wrote in the name of king Ahasuerus, and sealed it with the king's ring, and sent letters by posts on horseback, riding on swift steeds that were used in the king's service: wherein the king granted the Jews which were in every city to gather themselves together, and to stand for their life, to destroy, to slay, and to cause to perish, all the power of the people and province that would assault them, their little ones and women, and to take the spoil of them for a prey, upon one day in all the provinces of king Ahasuerus, namely, upon the thirteenth day of the twelfth month, which is the month Adar. So the posts that rode upon swift steeds that were used in the king's service went out, being hastened and pressed on by the king's commandment.

And Mordecai went forth from the presence of the king in royal apparel of blue and white, and with a great crown of gold, and with a robe of fine linen and purple: and the city of Shushan shouted and was glad. The Jews had light and gladness, and joy and honour. And in every province and in every city, whithersoever the king's commandment and his decree came, the Jews had gladness and joy, a feast and a good day. And many from among the peoples of the land became Jews; for the fear of the Jews was fallen upon them.

Now in the twelfth month, which is the month Adar, on the thirteenth day of the same, when the king's commandment and his decree drew near to be put in execution, in the day that the enemies of the Jews hoped to have rule over them; whereas it was turned to the contrary, that the Jews had rule over them that hated them; the Jews gathered themselves together in their cities throughout all the provinces of the king Ahasuerus, to lay hand on such as sought their hurt: and no man could withstand them; for the fear of them was fallen upon all the peoples. And all the princes of the provinces, and the satraps, and the governors, and they that did the king's business, helped the Jews; because the fear of Mordecai was fallen upon them. And the Jews that were in Shushan gathered themselves together on the fourteenth day also of the month Adar, and slew three hundred men in Shushan; but on the spoil they laid not their hand. And the other Jews that were in the king's provinces gathered themselves together, and stood for their lives, and had rest from their enemies, and slew of them that hated them seventy and five thousand; but on the spoil they laid not their hand.

This was done on the thirteenth day of the month Adar; and on the fourteenth day of the same they rested, and made it a day of feasting and gladness. But the Jews that were in Shushan assembled together on the thirteenth day thereof, and on the fourteenth thereof; and on the fifteenth day of the same they rested, and made it a day of feasting and gladness. Therefore do the Jews of the villages, that dwell in the unwalled towns, make the fourteenth day of the month Adar a day of gladness and feasting, and a good day, and of sending portions one to another.

iii

Stories of the Return

How Nehemiah rebuilt the Walls of Jerusalem

Now it came to pass in the month of Chislev, in the twentieth year, as I was in Shushan the palace, that Hanani, one of my brethren, came, he and certain men out of Judah; and I asked them concerning the Jews that had escaped, which were left of the captivity, and concerning Jerusalem. And they said unto me, The remnant that are left of the captivity there in the province are in great affliction and reproach: the wall of Jerusalem also is broken down, and the gates thereof are burned with fire. And it came to pass, when I heard these words, that I sat down and wept, and mourned certain days; and I fasted and prayed before the God of heaven, and said, I beseech thee, O LORD, the God of heaven, the great and terrible God, that keepeth covenant and mercy with them that love him and keep his commandments: let thine ear now be attentive, and thine eyes open, that thou mayest hearken unto the prayer of thy servant, which I pray before thee at this time, day and night, for the children of Israel thy servants, while I confess the sins of the children of Israel, which we have sinned against thee: yea, I and my father's house have sinned. We have dealt very corruptly against thee, and have not kept the commandments, nor the statutes, nor the judgements, which thou commandedst thy servant Moses. Remember, I beseech thee, the word that thou commandedst thy servant Moses, saying: 'If ye trespass, I will scatter you abroad among the peoples: but if ye return unto me, and keep my commandments and do them, though your outcasts were in the uttermost part of the heaven, yet will I gather them from thence, and will bring them unto the place that I have chosen to cause my name to dwell there.' Now these are thy servants and thy people, whom thou hast redeemed by thy great power, and by thy strong hand. O LORD, I beseech thee, let now thine ear be attentive to the prayer of thy servant, and to the prayer of thy servants, who delight to fear thy name: and prosper, I pray thee, thy servant this day, and grant him mercy in the sight of this man. (Now I was cupbearer to the king.)

And it came to pass in the month Nisan, in the twentieth year of Artaxerxes the king, when wine was before him, that I took up the wine, and gave it unto the king. Now I had not been beforetime sad in his presence. And the king said unto me, Why is thy countenance sad, seeing thou art not sick? this is nothing else but sorrow of heart. Then I was very sore afraid. And I said unto the king, Let the king live for ever: why should not my countenance be sad, when the city, the place of my fathers' sepulchres,

Nehemiah   Bible Stories

lieth waste, and the gates thereof are consumed with fire? Then the king said unto me, For what dost thou make request? So I prayed to the God of heaven. And I said unto the king, If it please the king, and if thy servant have found favour in thy sight, that thou wouldest send me unto Judah, unto the city of my fathers' sepulchres, that I may build it. And the king said unto me, (the queen also sitting by him,) For how long shall thy journey be? and when wilt thou return? So it pleased the king to send me; and I set him a time. Moreover I said unto the king, If it please the king, let letters be given me to the governors beyond the river, that they may let me pass through till I come unto Judah; and a letter unto Asaph the keeper of the king's forest, that he may give me timber to make beams for the gates of the castle which appertaineth to the house, and for the wall of the city, and for the house that I shall enter into. And the king granted me, according to the good hand of my God upon me.

 Then I came to the governors beyond the river, and gave them the king's letters. Now the king had sent with me captains of the army and horsemen. And when Sanballat the Horonite, and Tobiah the servant, the Ammonite, heard of it, it grieved them exceedingly, for that there was come a man to seek the welfare of the children of Israel. So I came to Jerusalem, and was there three days. And I arose in the night, I and some few men with me; neither told I any man what my God put into my heart to do for Jerusalem: neither was there any beast with me, save the beast that I rode upon. And I went out by night by the valley gate, even toward the dragon's well, and to the dung gate, and viewed the walls of Jerusalem, which were broken down, and the gates thereof were consumed with fire. Then I went on to the fountain gate and to the king's pool: but there was no place for the beast that was under me to pass. Then went I up in the night by the brook, and viewed the wall; and I turned back, and entered by the valley gate, and so returned. And the rulers knew not whither I went, or what I did; neither had I as yet told it to the Jews, nor to the priests, nor to the nobles, nor to the rulers, nor to the rest that did the work. Then said I unto them, Ye see the evil case that we are in, how Jerusalem lieth waste, and the gates thereof are burned with fire: come and let us build up the wall of Jerusalem, that we be no more a reproach. And I told them of the hand of my God which was good upon me; as also of the king's words that he had spoken unto me. And they said, Let us rise up and build. So they strengthened their hands for the good work.

But it came to pass that, when Sanballat heard that we builded the wall, he was wroth, and took great indignation, and mocked the Jews. And he spake before his brethren and the army of Samaria, and said, What do these feeble Jews? will they fortify themselves? will they sacrifice? will they make an end in a day? will they revive the stones out of the heaps of rubbish, seeing they are burned? Now Tobiah the Ammonite was by him, and he said, Even that which they build, if a fox go up, he shall break down their stone wall. (Hear, O our God; for we are despised: and turn back their reproach upon their own head, and give them up to spoiling in a land of captivity: and cover not their iniquity, and let not their sin be blotted out from before thee: for they have provoked thee to anger before the builders.) So we built the wall; and all the wall was joined together unto half the height thereof: for the people had a mind to work.

But it came to pass that, when Sanballat, and Tobiah, and the Arabians, and the Ammonites, and the Ashdodites, heard that the repairing of the walls of Jerusalem went forward, and that the breaches began to be stopped, then they were very wroth; and they conspired all of them together to come and fight against Jerusalem, and to cause confusion therein. But we made our prayer unto our God, and set a watch against them day and night, because of them. And Judah said, The strength of the bearers of burdens is decayed, and there is much rubbish: so that we are not able to build the wall. And our adversaries said, They shall not know, neither see, till we come into the midst of them, and slay them, and cause the work to cease. And it came to pass that, when the Jews which dwelt by them came, they said unto us ten times

Exile and Return ❧ Nehemiah

from all places, Ye must return unto us. Therefore set I in the lowest parts of the space behind the wall, in the open places, I even set the people after their families with their swords, their spears, and their bows. And I looked, and rose up, and said unto the nobles, and to the rulers, and to the rest of the people, Be not ye afraid of them: remember the Lord, which is great and terrible, and fight for your brethren, your sons and your daughters, your wives and your houses. And it came to pass, when our enemies heard that it was known unto us, and God had brought their counsel to nought, that we returned all of us to the wall, every one unto his work. And it came to pass from that time forth, that half of my servants wrought in the work, and half of them held the spears, the shields, and the bows, and the coats of mail; and the rulers were behind all the house of Judah. They that builded the wall and they that bare burdens laded themselves, every one with one of his hands wrought in the work, and with the other held his weapon; and the builders, every one had his sword girded by his side, and so builded. And he that sounded the trumpet was by me. And I said unto the nobles, and to the rulers and to the rest of the people, The work is great and large, and we are separated upon the wall, one far from another: in what place soever ye hear the sound of the trumpet, resort ye thither unto us; our God shall fight for us. So we wrought in the work: and half of them held the spears from the rising of the morning till the stars appeared. Likewise at the same time said I unto the people, Let every one with his servant lodge within Jerusalem, that in the night they may be a guard to us, and may labour in the day. So neither I, nor my brethren, nor my servants, nor the men of the guard which followed me, none of us put off our clothes, every one went with his weapon to the water.

Now it came to pass, when it was reported to Sanballat and Tobiah, and to Geshem the Arabian, and unto the rest of our enemies, that I had builded the wall, and that there was no breach left therein; (though even unto that time I had not set up the doors in the gates;) that Sanballat and Geshem sent unto me, saying, Come, let us meet together in one of the villages in the plain of Ono. But they thought to do me mischief. And I sent messengers unto them, saying, I am doing a great work, so that I cannot come down: why should the work cease, whilst I leave it, and come down to you? And they sent unto me four times after this sort; and I answered them after the same manner. Then sent Sanballat his servant unto me in like manner the fifth time with an open letter in his hand; wherein was written, It is reported among the nations, and Gashmu saith it, that thou and the Jews think to rebel; for which cause thou buildest the wall: and thou wouldest be their king, according to these words. And thou hast also appointed prophets to preach of thee at Jerusalem, saying, There is a king in Judah: and now shall it be reported to the king according to these words. Come now therefore, and let us take counsel together. Then I sent unto him, saying, There are no such things done as thou sayest, but thou feignest them out of thine own heart. For they all would have made us afraid, saying, Their hands shall be weakened from the work, that it be not done. But now, O God, strengthen thou my hands.

And I went unto the house of Shemaiah who was shut up; and he said, Let us meet together in the house of God, within the temple, and let us shut the doors of the temple: for they will come to slay thee; yea, in the night will they come to slay thee. And I said, Should such a man as I flee? and who is there, that, being such as I, would go into the temple to save his life? I will not go in. And I discerned, and, lo, God had not sent him: but he pronounced this prophecy against me: and Tobiah and Sanballat had hired him. For this cause was he hired, that I should be afraid, and do so, and sin, and that they might have matter for an evil report, that they might reproach me. Remember, O my God, Tobiah and Sanballat according to these their works, and also the prophetess Noadiah, and the rest of the prophets, that would have put me in fear.

So the wall was finished in the twenty and fifth day of the month Elul, in fifty and two days. And it came to pass, when all our enemies heard thereof, that all the heathen that were about us feared, and were much cast down in their own eyes: for they perceived that this work was wrought of our God.

And at the dedication of the wall of Jerusalem they sought the Levites out of all their places, to bring them to Jerusalem, to keep the dedication with gladness, both with thanksgivings, and with singing, with cymbals, psalteries, and with harps. And the sons of the singers gathered themselves together, both out of the plain round about Jerusalem, and from the villages. Then I brought up the princes of Judah upon the wall, and appointed two great companies that gave thanks and went in procession. Whereof one went on the right hand upon the wall toward the dung gate: (and Ezra the scribe was before them:) and by the fountain gate, and straight before them, they went up by the stairs of the city of David, at the going up of the wall, above the house of David, even unto the water gate eastward. And the other company of them that gave thanks went to meet them, and I after them, with the half of the people, upon the wall, above the tower of the furnaces, even unto the broad wall; and above the gate of Ephraim, and by the old gate, and by the fish gate, and the tower of Hananel, and the tower of Hammeah, even unto the sheep gate: and they stood still in the gate of the guard. So stood the two companies of them that gave thanks in the house of God, and I, and the half of the rulers with me. And the singers sang loud, with

Jezrahiah their overseer. And they offered great sacrifices that day, and rejoiced; for God had made them rejoice with great joy; and the women also and the children rejoiced: so that the joy of Jerusalem was heard even afar off.

The Renewal of the Covenant under Ezra

And when the seventh month was come, the children of Israel were in their cities. And all the people gathered themselves together as one man into the broad place that was before the water gate; and they spake unto Ezra the scribe to bring the book of the law of Moses, which the LORD had commanded to Israel. And Ezra the priest brought the law before the congregation, both men and women, and all that could hear with understanding, upon the first day of the seventh month. And he read therein before the broad place that was before the water gate from early morning until midday, in the presence of the men and the women, and of those that could understand; and the ears of all the people were attentive unto the book of the law. And Ezra the scribe stood upon a pulpit of wood, which they had made for the purpose. And Ezra opened the book in the sight of all the people; (for he was above all the people;) and when he opened it, all the people stood up: and Ezra blessed the LORD, the great God. And all the people answered, Amen, Amen, with the lifting up of their hands: and they bowed their heads, and worshipped the LORD with their faces to the ground. Also the Levites caused the people to understand the law: and the people stood in their place. And they read in the book, in the law of God, distinctly; and they gave the sense, so that they understood the reading. And Nehemiah, which was the Tirshatha, and Ezra the priest the scribe, and the Levites that taught the people, said unto all the people, This day is holy unto the LORD your God; mourn not, nor weep. For all the people wept, when they heard the words of the law. Then he said unto them, Go your way, eat the fat, and drink the sweet, and send portions unto him for whom nothing is prepared: for this day is holy unto our LORD: neither be ye grieved; for the joy of the LORD is your strength. So the Levites stilled all the people, saying, Hold your peace, for the day is holy; neither be ye grieved. And all the people went their way to eat, and to drink, and to send portions, and to make great mirth, because they had understood the words that were declared unto them.

Now in the twenty and fourth day of this month the children of Israel were assembled with fasting, and with sackcloth, and earth upon them. And the seed of Israel separated themselves from all strangers, and stood and confessed their sins, and the iniquities of their fathers. And they stood up in their place, and read in the book of the law of the LORD their God a fourth part of the day;

and another fourth part they confessed, and worshipped the LORD their God. Then the Levites said:

"Stand up and bless the LORD your God from everlasting to everlasting: and blessed be thy glorious name, which is exalted above all blessing and praise. Thou art the LORD, even thou alone; thou hast made heaven, the heaven of heavens, with all their host, the earth and all things that are thereon, the seas and all that is in them, and thou preservest them all; and the host of heaven worshippeth thee. Thou art the LORD the God, who didst choose Abram, and broughtest him forth out of Ur of the Chaldees, and gavest him the name of Abraham; and foundest his heart faithful before thee, and madest a covenant with him to give the land of the Canaanite, the Hittite, the Amorite, and the Perizzite, and the Jebusite, and the Girgashite, even to give it unto his seed, and hast performed thy words; for thou art righteous. And thou sawest the affliction of our fathers in Egypt, and heardest their cry by the Red Sea; and shewedst signs and wonders upon Pharaoh, and on all his servants, and on all the people of his land; for thou knewest that they dealt proudly against them; and didst get thee a name, as it is this day. And thou didst divide the sea before them, so that they went through the midst of the sea on the dry land; and their pursuers thou didst cast into the depths, as a stone into the mighty waters. Moreover thou leddest them in a pillar of cloud by day;

and in a pillar of fire by night, to give them light in the way wherein they should go. Thou camest down also upon mount Sinai, and spakest with them from heaven, and gavest them right judgements and true laws, good statutes and commandments: and madest known unto them thy holy sabbath, and commandedst them commandments, and statutes, and a law, by the hand of Moses thy servant; and gavest them bread from heaven for their hunger, and broughtest forth water for them out of the rock for their thirst, and commandedst them that they should go in to possess the land which thou hadst lifted up thine hand to give them. But they and our fathers dealt proudly, and hardened their neck, and hearkened not to thy commandments, and refused to obey, neither were mindful of thy wonders that thou didst among them; but hardened their neck, and in their rebellion appointed a captain to return to their bondage: but thou art a God ready to pardon, gracious and full of compassion, slow to anger, and plenteous in mercy, and forsookest them not. Yea, when they had made them a molten calf, and said, This is thy God that brought thee up out of Egypt, and had wrought great provocations; yet thou in thy manifold mercies forsookest them not in the wilderness: the pillar of cloud departed not from over them by day, to lead them in the way; neither the pillar of fire by night, to shew them light, and the way wherein they should go. Thou gavest also thy good spirit to instruct them, and withheldest not thy

Exile and Return — Ezra

manna from their mouth, and gavest them water for their thirst. Yea, forty years didst thou sustain them in the wilderness, and they lacked nothing; their clothes waxed not old, and their feet swelled not. Moreover thou gavest them kingdoms and peoples, which thou didst allot after their portions: so they possessed the land of Sihon, even the land of the king of Heshbon, and the land of Og king of Bashan. Their children also multipliedst thou as the stars of heaven, and broughtest them into the land, concerning which thou didst say to their fathers, that they should go in to possess it. So the children went in and possessed the land, and thou subduedst before them the inhabitants of the land, the Canaanites, and gavest them into their hands, with their kings, and the peoples of the land, that they might do with them as they would. And they took fenced cities, and a fat land, and possessed houses full of all good things, cisterns hewn out, vineyards, and oliveyards, and fruit trees in abundance: so they did eat, and were filled, and became fat, and delighted themselves in thy great goodness. Nevertheless they were disobedient, and rebelled against thee, and cast thy law behind their back, and slew thy prophets which testified against them to turn them again unto thee, and they wrought great provocations. Therefore thou deliveredst them into the hand of their adversaries, who distressed them: and in the time of their trouble, when they cried unto thee, thou heardest from heaven; and according to thy manifold mercies thou gavest them saviours who saved them out of the hand of their adversaries. But after they had rest, they did evil again before thee: therefore leftest thou them in the hand of their enemies, so that they had the dominion over them: yet when they returned, and cried unto thee, thou heardest from heaven; and many times didst thou deliver them according to thy mercies; and testifiedst against them, that thou mightest bring them again unto thy law: yet they dealt proudly, and hearkened not unto thy commandments, but sinned against thy judgements, (which if a man do, he shall live in them,) and withdrew the shoulder, and hardened their neck, and would not hear. Yet many years didst thou bear with them, and testifiedst against them by thy spirit through thy prophets: yet would they not give ear: therefore gavest thou them into the hand of the peoples of the lands. Nevertheless in thy manifold mercies thou didst not make a full end of them, nor forsake them; for thou art a gracious and merciful God.

"Now therefore, our God, the great, the mighty, and the terrible God, who keepest covenant and mercy, let not all the travail seem little before thee, that hath come upon us, on our kings, on our princes, and on our priests, and on our prophets, and on our fathers, and on all thy people, since the time of the kings of Assyria unto this day. Howbeit thou art just in all that is come upon us; for thou hast dealt truly, but we have done wickedly:

neither have our kings, our princes, our priests, nor our fathers, kept thy law, nor hearkened unto thy commandments and thy testimonies, wherewith thou didst testify against them. For they have not served thee in their kingdom, and in thy great goodness that thou gavest them, and in the large and fat land which thou gavest before them, neither turned they from their wicked works. Behold, we are servants this day, and as for the land that thou gavest unto our fathers to eat the fruit thereof and the good thereof, behold, we are servants in it. And it yieldeth much increase unto the kings whom thou hast set over us because of our sins: also they have power over our bodies, and over our cattle, at their pleasure, and we are in great distress. And yet for all this we make a sure covenant, and write it; and our princes, our Levites, and our priests, seal unto it."

And the people, the priests, the Levites, the porters, the singers, the Nethinim, and all they that had separated themselves from the peoples of the lands unto the law of God, their wives, their sons, and their daughters, every one that had knowledge and understanding; they clave to their brethren, their nobles, and entered into a curse, and into an oath, "to walk in God's law, which was given by Moses the servant of God, and to observe and do all the commandments of the LORD our Lord, and his judgements and his statutes; and that we would not give our daughters unto the peoples of the land, nor take their daughters for our sons: and if the peoples of the land bring ware or any victuals on the sabbath day to sell, that we would not buy of them on the sabbath, or on a holy day: and that we would forgo the seventh year, and the exaction of every debt."

Exile and Return ❧ Notes

Notes to the Exile and Return

Page 259. *Threescore cubits:* the *cubit* was the length of the average man's arm, from elbow to wrist.

Page 263. '*Nebuchadnezzar, the king, unto all the peoples*, etc.' It will be seen that this story is told in the form of the actual proclamation made by Nebuchadnezzar concerning the wonderful thing that happened to him.

Page 263. *Magicians, enchanters, Chaldeans, soothsayers,* all mean much the same thing. *Sooth* is an old word for *truth*; *soothsayers* professed to read the truth of coming events in the stars, or in dreams, or by other means. The Chaldean nation (of which Babylon was the capital) was so far ahead of other peoples in this power of interpreting secrets that the word *Chaldeans* was used as meaning *soothsayers*.

Page 264. *Behold, a watcher and an holy one came down from heaven:* these are names for angels. *Watcher* survives in the modern term *Guardian Angel*.

Page 266. *And seven times shall pass over thee:* the interpretation of the dream does not tell everything: it might be seven days, or seven months, or seven years, or seven of any other period.

Page 270. *Shall rule as one of three:* shall be made a member of a council of three, to rule the state under the king.

Page 271. One reason why the other wise men could not make out the writing on the wall was that they tried to read it in the usual way, *across;* and they could make no words of the letters. Daniel sees that it must be read *down, up, down,* — an old form of writing, called (in Greek) *boustrophedon,* that is, the way an ox draws a plough, turning at the end of the furrow and going back. As soon as Daniel suggests this, all can read the words *Mene, mene, tekel, upharsin. Mene* means number; *tekel* weight; *peres* division. But only Daniel sees what the words mean when put together.

Page 278. *Mordecai sat in the king's gate:* in eastern life the gate of a city or palace is like a modern city hall; persons linger about it to have their affairs taken up by kings or magistrates. Even now the Turkish court is called the Sublime *Porte* (gate).

Page 278. *Haman the Agagite:* this is another word for Amalekite. Haman thus belonged to a nation that was always the foe of Israel (compare Story ix in *The Judges*).

Page 282. *Let the king and Haman come ... unto the banquet which I have prepared.* Esther has to contend against the power of the court favourite, Haman, and has nothing on her side except her wonderful beauty. Thus her motive in inviting to these banquets is to get time for her beauty to be more and more felt by the king, before she reveals her purpose against Haman.

Page 285. *But if we had been sold for bondmen and bondwomen,* etc. Esther knows human nature too well to trust merely to the king's compassion. She hints in these words at something which was too often forgotten in old times — how that the loss of subjects' lives (for example, in war) is so much loss to the wealth of the kingdom, and therefore loss to the

Exile and Return   Notes

sovereign. Had the Jewish nation been sold into slavery (she says), there would have been a price to set against the loss of subjects, but when they are slain there is not even this. *Although the adversary could not have compensated for the king's damage:* an allusion to Haman's offer of ten thousand talents (above, p. 279), which had been made known to her by Mordecai. In the light of this new idea — that the death of subjects is loss to the king — what had before seemed a magnificent bribe of Haman now appears a paltry sum to set against a whole nation of subjects.

Page 292. *Sanballat the Heronite, Tobiah the servant, the Ammonite:* these were officials, representing the Babylonian or Persian government in the conquered country of Judea. The persons appointed to these offices would be chosen by the conquerors from the nations who had been neighbours and enemies of the Jews; hence their hostility to Nehemiah's project of rebuilding Jerusalem.

Page 294. *And Judah said:* that is, the very Jews who were working with Nehemiah became discouraged. — *The Jews which dwelt by them . . . said . . . Ye must return unto us.* Many companies of Jewish exiles had been allowed to return to the land of Judea; but Nehemiah was the first to attempt the restoration of Jerusalem as a fortress. The timid Jewish exiles here want Nehemiah to give up his plan, and live in the country like themselves.

Page 300. *Nehemiah . . . the Tirshatha:* this is a Persian word: he had been appointed governor of Jerusalem under the Persian king. — *Ezra, the scribe:* the word *scribe* has great importance at this period of history. It does not merely mean (as in modern English) a *writer*, but a teacher of the *written law*.

Page 305. *The Nethinim* (a plural word) : some division of sacred officials, the meaning of which is not clearly known.

Small 18mo. Cloth extra, 50 cents each; Leather, 60 cents.

The Modern Reader's Bible.

A Series of Books from the Sacred Scriptures,
presented in Modern Literary Form,

BY

RICHARD G. MOULTON,

M.A. (Camb.), Ph.D. (Penn.),

Professor of Literature in English in the University of Chicago.

PRESS COMMENTS.

The Outlook, New York. "The effect of these changes back to the original forms under which the sacred writings first appeared will be, for the vast majority of readers, a surprise and delight; they will feel as if they had come upon new spiritual and intellectual treasures, and they will appreciate for the first time how much the Bible has suffered from the hands of those who have treated it without reference to its literary quality. In view of the significance and possible results of Professor Moulton's undertaking, it is not too much to pronounce it one of the most important spiritual and literary events of the times. It is part of the renaissance of Biblical study; but it may mean, and in our judgment it does mean, the renewal of a fresh and deep impression of the beauty and power of the supreme spiritual writing of the world."

Presbyterian and Reformed Review. "Unquestionably here is a task worth carrying out: and it is to be said at once that Dr. Moulton has carried it out with great skill and helpfulness. Both the introduction and the notes are distinct contributions to the better understanding and higher appreciation of the literary character, features and beauties of the Biblical books treated."

THE MACMILLAN COMPANY
66 FIFTH AVENUE, NEW YORK

WISDOM SERIES

IN FOUR VOLUMES

THE PROVERBS
A Miscellany of Sayings and Poems embodying Isolated Observations of Life.

ECCLESIASTICUS
A Miscellany including longer compositions, still embodying only Isolated Observations of Life.

ECCLESIASTES — WISDOM OF SOLOMON
Each is a Series of Connected Writings embodying, from different standpoints, a Solution of the Whole Mystery of Life.

THE BOOK OF JOB
A Dramatic Poem in which are embodied Varying Solutions of the Mystery of Life.

DEUTERONOMY
The Orations and Songs of Moses, constituting his Farewell to the People of Israel.

BIBLICAL IDYLS
The Lyric Idyl of Solomon's Song, and the Epic Idyls of Ruth, Esther, and Tobit.

THE PSALMS (Two Volumes)
Containing the whole of The Psalms and also the Book of Lamentations.

SELECT MASTERPIECES OF BIBLICAL LITERATURE

HISTORY SERIES

IN FIVE VOLUMES

GENESIS
Bible History, Part I : Formation of the Chosen Nation.

THE EXODUS
Bible History, Part II: Migration of the Chosen Nation to the Land of Promise. — Book of Exodus, with Leviticus and Numbers.

THE JUDGES
Bible History, Part III: The Chosen Nation in its Efforts towards Secular Government. — Books of Joshua, Judges, I Samuel.

THE KINGS
Bible History, Part IV: The Chosen Nation under a Secular Government side by side with a Theocracy. — Books of II Samuel, I and II Kings.

THE CHRONICLES
Ecclesiastical History of the Chosen Nation. — Books of Chronicles, Ezra, Nehemiah.

PROPHECY SERIES

IN FOUR VOLUMES

ISAIAH
The vision of Isaiah, the Son of Amoz, which he saw concerning Judah and Jerusalem in the days of Uzziah, Jotham, Ahaz, and Hezekiah, Kings of Judah.

EZEKIEL
The prophetic works of Ezekiel.

JEREMIAH
The words of Jeremiah, the Son of Hilkiah, to whom the Word of the Lord came in the days of Josiah, Jehoiakim, and Zedekiah, Kings of Judah.

DANIEL AND THE MINOR PROPHETS

Containing The Book of Daniel, The Prophecy of Hosea, The Prophecy of Joel, The Book of Amos, The Vision of Obadiah, The Book of Jonah, The Prophecy of Micah, The Oracle Concerning Nineveh and the Book of Nahum, The Oracle which Habakkuk did see, The Prophecy of Zephaniah, The Book of Haggai, The Book of Zechariah, and other anonymous prophecies.

NEW TESTAMENT SERIES

IN FOUR VOLUMES

ST. MATTHEW, ST. MARK, and the GENERAL EPISTLES

Containing The Gospel according to St. Matthew, The Gospel according to St. Mark, an Epistle to the Hebrews, The Epistle of St. James, The Epistles of St. Peter, and The Epistle of St. Jude.

ST. LUKE and ST. PAUL (Two Volumes)

Containing The Gospel of St. Luke, The Acts of the Apostles, with the Pauline Epistles introduced at the several points of the history to which they are usually referred. An opportunity will thus be afforded of studying, without the interruption of comment or discussion, the continuous History of the New Testament Church as presented by itself.

ST. JOHN

Containing the Gospel, Epistles, and Revelation of St. John.

THE MACMILLAN COMPANY
66 FIFTH AVENUE, NEW YORK

www.ingramcontent.com/pod-product-compliance
Lightning Source LLC
Chambersburg PA
CBHW021205230426
43667CB00006B/564